Classic CONVERTIBLES

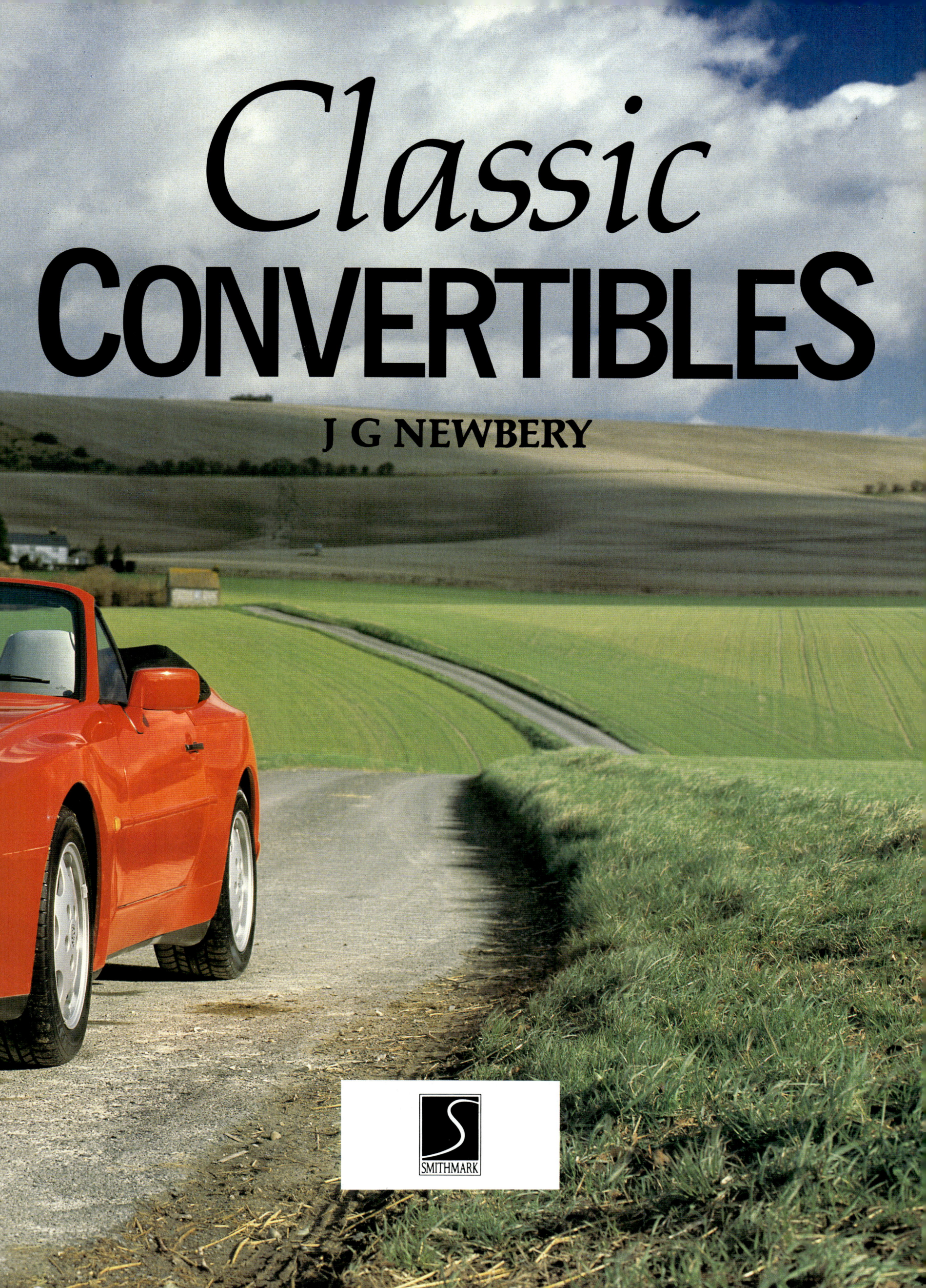

Copyright © 1994 Brompton Books Corp.

All rights reserved. No part of this publication may be reproduced, stored in a retrieval system or transmitted in any form by any means, electronic, mechanical, photocopying or otherwise, without first obtaining written permission of the copyright owner.

This edition published in 1995
by SMITHMARK Publishers Inc.
16 East 32nd Street
New York, New York 10016.

SMITHMARK books are available for bulk purchase for sales promotion and premium use. For details write or telephone the Manager of Special Sales, SMITHMARK Publishers Inc., 16 East 32nd Street, New York, NY 10016, (212) 532 6600

Produced by Brompton Books Corp.,
15 Sherwood Place,
Greenwich, CT 06830

ISBN 0-8317-1438-7

Printed in Spain

10 9 8 7 6 5 4 3 2

Page 1: To many people, the term 'convertible' automatically conjures up the vision of a sportscar like this 1973 Jaguar E-type, with its 5.3-liter V12 engine.

Pages 2-3: In recent years the convertible has undergone a revival of interest. This 1990 Porsche 944 cabriolet is representative of the modern sports convertible.

These pages: Not every convertible is a sporting car, of course. In the America of the early 1950s, a convertible Cadillac like this one was the ultimate owner-driver luxury car.

Contents

Introduction	6	The Italian Convertible	60
The Convertible Since 1945	8	The American Convertible	74
The British Convertible	20	The Japanese Convertible	94
The German Convertible	36	Index	112
The French Convertible	50	Acknowledgments	112

Introduction

Ever since the late 1920s, when it became customary for motor manufacturers to offer closed cars for sale instead of the open ones so characteristic of the early years of motoring, the convertible has enjoyed a special place in motorists' affections. The reason has partly been that convertibles have been made in smaller numbers than closed cars and therefore offer something out of the ordinary; but undoubtedly the main reason for the convertible's appeal is that it offers a sensual stimulus which no closed car can. There is nothing else quite like driving on an open road with the sun beating down on your back and the wind tearing at your hair.

Conversely, there is also nothing quite like an open car in the cold or the rain, and for that reason all but the most sporting of open cars have always offered some degree of weather protection. They have been, in a word, 'convertible' – from open to closed and back again at the whim of the owner.

The word 'convertible' is actually a shortened form of the term 'convertible coupe' and that, strictly, was a two-door car with four seats and a folding roof. It gained currency during the 1950s and 1960s, not least because it was a simple term with which to replace the variety of descriptions traditionally applied to 'convertible' cars. Until then, what the Americans called a convertible coupe was known as a drophead coupé in Britain and as a cabriolet on the European continent. Confusingly, a cabriolet in Britain was a four-door convertible car, which in turn was known in America as a convertible sedan! Such weird and wonderful variations as Surrey tops (by Triumph), Targa tops (by Porsche and others) and retractable hard tops (by Ford in America) would only have confused the issue further if the all-embracing term 'convertible' had not been available.

Today, therefore, 'convertible' covers a wide variety of different body styles – and even those small sedans which have roll-back or fold-back roofs (though not simple sunroofs) can be described as convertibles. But no car which has imperfect weather protection – such as the canvas sidescreens associated with British two-seaters until the end of the 1950s – can be properly described as 'convertible.' For that reason, such cars are not included in this book.

INTRODUCTION 7

Right: The Mercedes-Benz 170S cabriolet was built for only two seasons, from 1949 to 1951. With just 52bhp from its four-cylinder engine of 1767cc, it was by no means a high-performance car. Nevertheless, the quality which was always a Mercedes-Benz trademark made it a highly desirable piece of property. The prominent folded hood is typical of German designs of the period.

Below: With the advent of the Mark II convertible model in 1962, Austin turned its Austin-Healey 3000 from a roadster with sidescreens into a sporting convertible with proper weather protection. The big Healeys had 2.9-liter six-cylinder engines, and could reach 117mph, even in standard trim.

The Convertible Since 1945

THE CONVERTIBLE SINCE 1945

In the period after 1945, which nowadays is the one most attractive to car enthusiasts, the products of motor manufacturers commonly betrayed what can best be called national characteristics. The motor-taxation policies of a country, the kind of roads it had, and the sort of use to which its inhabitants commonly put their cars, all had an effect on the type of cars that its domestic manufacturers produced. Thus Swedish manufacturers did not make open cars (which would have had limited appeal in a predominantly cold climate), while Italian and French manufacturers tended to concentrate on smaller-engined cars because of heavy taxation on large engines in their home markets. It was not until the 1970s that these national characteristics began to play a less important role.

It was the need to export which brought about the growth of the international, as distinct from the national, car – and this affected convertibles just as much as other types. Exports had been of far less concern during the 1930s than they became after World War II, when the European manufacturers found their home markets economically unstable and therefore unable to absorb all the cars they could make. In order to survive they looked for export markets, and before long recognized that they needed to adapt the national characteristics of their products to suit the needs and expectations of customers in these export markets. As a result there was a gradual leveling process and, within 30 years, manufacturers were generally producing cars which had appeal in a wide spectrum of markets. Inevitably, this meant that cars from different nations came to have what were essentially the same characteristics.

One very significant factor in this leveling process was the importance of the American market. When the European manufacturers began to look for

Previous pages: Typical of the British middle-class touring convertible of the early 1950s is this Armstrong Siddeley Hurricane drophead coupe.

Left: The first of the Aston Martin DB series cars to go on sale was the DB1 of 1948. It had a 2-liter four-cylinder engine and came as either a tourer or a drophead coupe.

Right: Humber's large and luxurious Super Snipe was rare in convertible form. This is a 1954 example, with three-position drophead-coupe bodywork by Tickford.

Below: There were attractive convertible versions of many mass-produced sedans in the 1950s, such as this Ford Zephyr 6 of 1954.

Left: A passenger's-eye view of a mid-1960s Aston Martin DB5 drophead coupe. These cars were exclusive sporting models, which offered high performance and superb quality of build.

Below left: There has always been something special about a Ferrari, and particularly about an open Ferrari. The 2.9-liter V12 engine in this 250GT spyder was capable of propelling the car to speeds of around 140mph, which was heady stuff for the late 1950s and early 1960s.

Above right: The original Mercedes-Benz 300SL was a coupe, but the prospect of large sales in sunny California persuaded its German manufacturer to replace it with a convertible in 1957. Confusingly, this was known as a roadster, even though it came with proper weather protection for the occupants.

Below right: The Chevrolet Corvette was one of America's favorite open sportscars in 1962, when this example was built. The engine was a 327 cubic-inch V8.

new export markets in the late 1940s, many of them turned to the United States, for that country had emerged from World War II with a healthy economy and was able and willing to buy foreign cars. For many years the American market was content to accept the different characteristics of convertibles from Britain, from Germany, or from Italy. However, the introduction of legislation during the late 1960s which affected every new car sold in the United States forced manufacturers who sold their cars there to meet a common set of standards.

Just how important the American market had become for some of these manufacturers became crystal-clear at the same time. None of them wanted to be denied the opportunity of selling their products in the world's largest and most lucrative car market, and all of them began to develop new designs or to adapt existing ones to meet the new standards. These standards both governed permitted levels of noxious gases in car exhausts and set new requirements for occupant safety. It was this latter legislation which was to have a major impact on the history of the convertible.

By the end of the 1960s it seemed certain that further legislation during the 1970s would ban the sale of open cars in the United States, on the grounds that occupants would not be protected from injury by a fabric roof (or indeed by no roof at all) if the car rolled over in an accident. The widespread expectation of this legislation had a dramatic effect on manu-

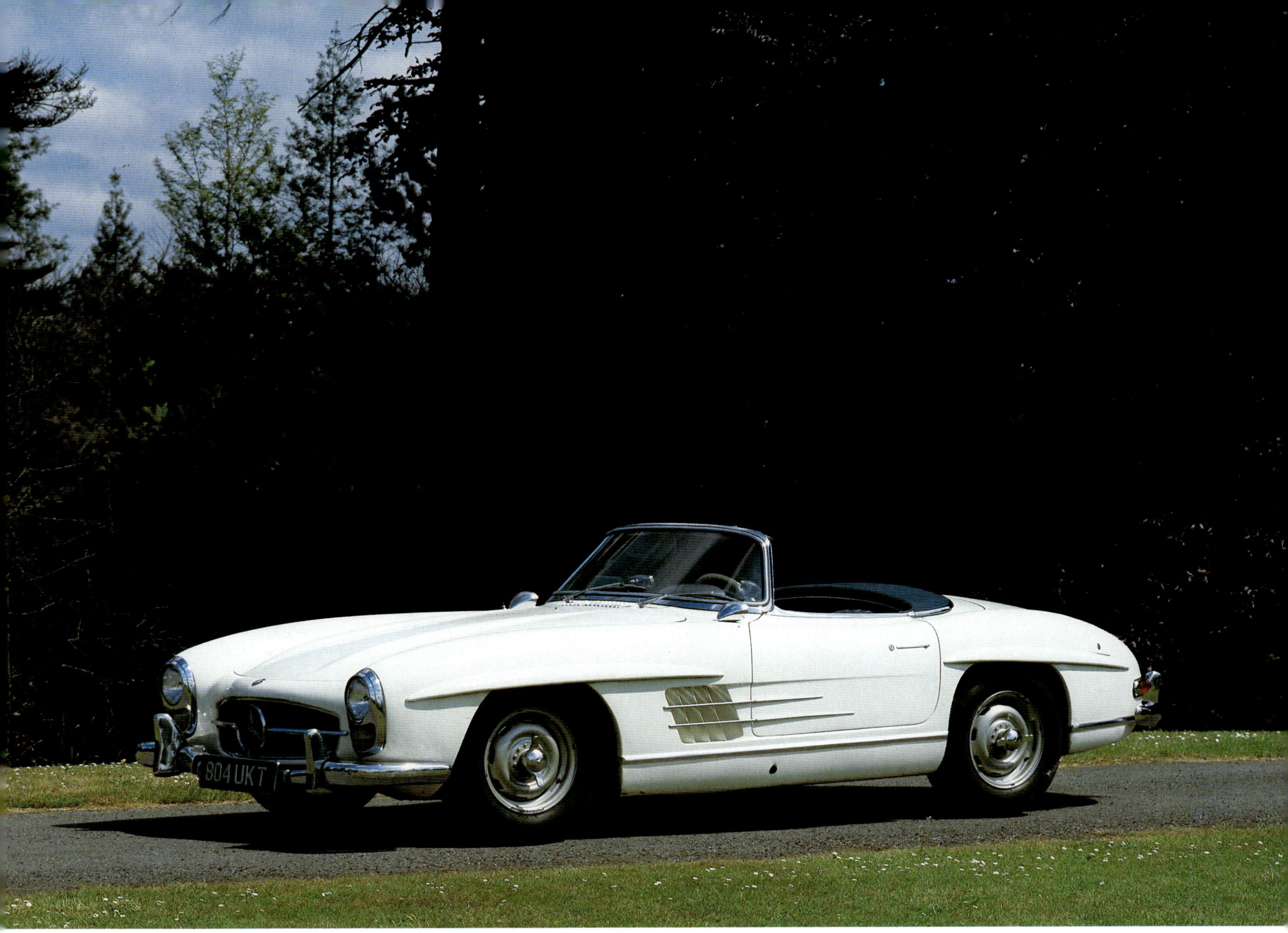
804 UKT

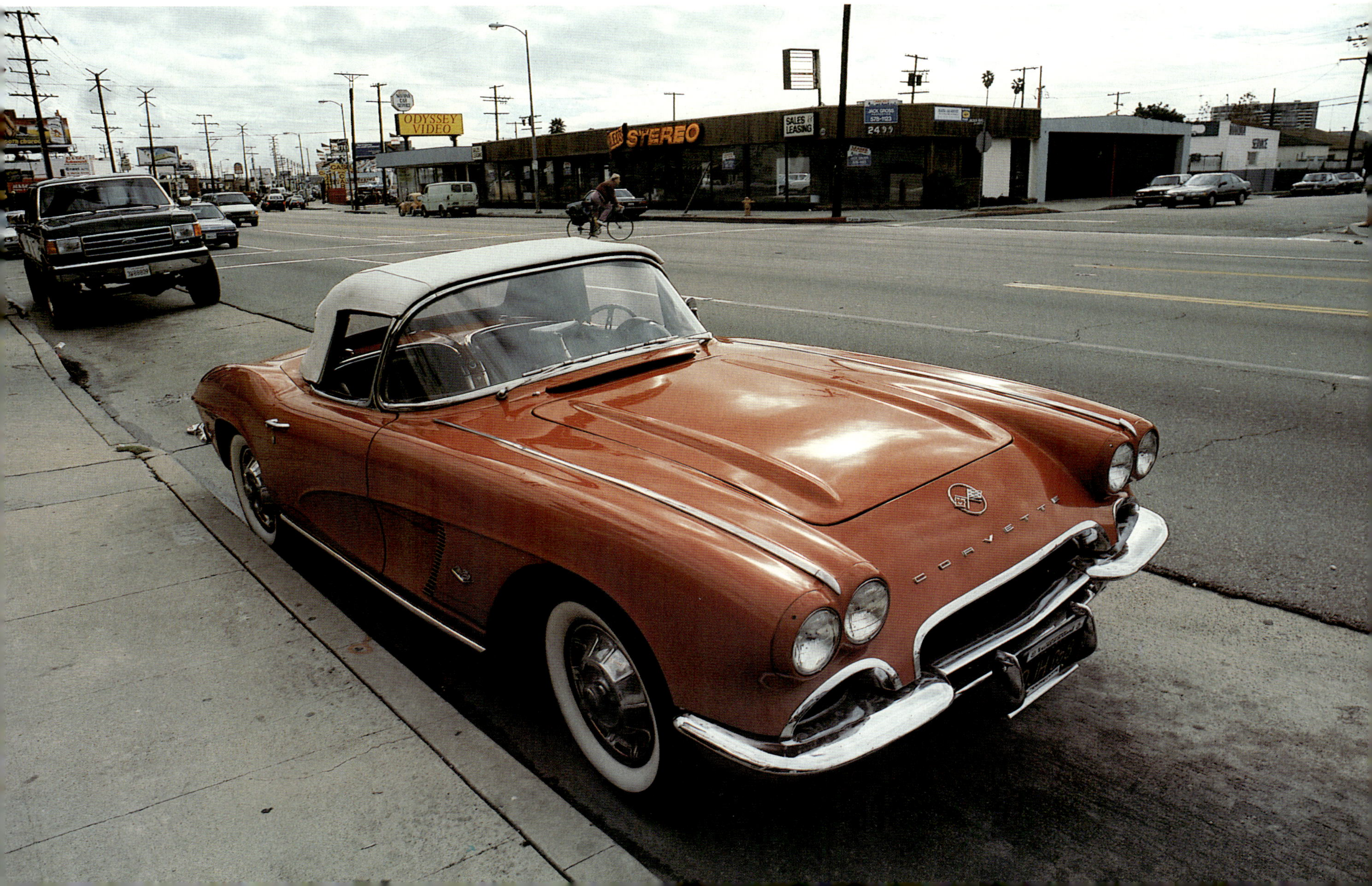
ODYSSEY
VIDEO
STEREO
CORVETTE

This page: Top, a 1963 Triumph TR4 sportscar, which offered 100mph-plus performance. *Left,* a luxurious 1963 Rolls-Royce Silver Cloud III drophead coupe, with the gorgeous 'Chinese Eye' body style. Where the Triumph had a 'Surrey top', the Rolls-Royce had a power-operated convertible top.

Above right: When safety became a major consideration for car makers in the late 1960s, new types of open car began to appear. Typical of the times was the Triumph Stag, which had a rigid 'T-bar' over the passenger compartment to protect the occupants in a rollover accident.

Below right: One of the most coveted Ferraris is the Daytona spyder, the open version of the V12-engined 365 GTB/4, with bodywork by Pininfarina. Only 50 genuine spyders were built.

THE CONVERTIBLE SINCE 1945   17

Left: The Lea Francis 3.5-liter convertible of 1980 attempted to revive an old British name. It combined modern mechanical elements with a handbuilt body whose styling drew on the fashions of the 1940s and 1950s.

Right: Swedish manufacturers did not generally indulge in open cars, for which there was almost no domestic market. Lured by the prospect of sales in the USA, however, SAAB introduced this attractive cabriolet version of its 900 turbo sedan in the 1980s.

Below: BMW explored the market for a two-seater convertible in the late 1980s, but the Z1 was too expensive to succeed as anything more than an exclusive limited edition.

facturers' product-development programs worldwide. For those who made convertibles, the United States was without question their largest market and, if convertibles became unsaleable there, it was doubtful whether sales elsewhere would justify the cost of developing new convertible models. Worse, there was a good chance that other countries might follow the United States' example and ban the sale of open cars, thus making such vehicles virtually unsaleable anywhere in the world. Against the background of commercial considerations like these, it is scarcely surprising that manufacturers worldwide introduced no new convertibles until the end of the 1970s, by which time the threat of legislation banning open cars in the United States had passed.

Even then the market for convertibles took a very long time to recover. The rest of the world largely followed America's lead – because of the importance to manufacturers everywhere of the American market – and many of the open cars of the early 1980s were, in fact, Targa-top models, with rigid structural elements above the occupants' heads to allay fears about safety in a rollover accident. By the end of the 1980s, however, it did look as though the fully-open, fabric-roof convertible might be returning to favor; and a number of new convertible models from manufacturers worldwide was evidence that the car makers had confidence in the future of the open car once again.

But the leveling process had taken its toll. By the beginning of the 1980s it

18 CLASSIC CONVERTIBLES

was hard to identify most convertibles' country of origin. Even American models had shrunk to the same size as their European counterparts, and styling details were no longer a wholly reliable guide to American origin. The majority of the new convertibles of the 1980s had characteristics intended to have an international appeal, and in fact many had been developed in more than one country: some Japanese convertibles, for example, had been partly developed in the United States, while European Fords were the joint products of British and German design departments. Even Sweden, which had never needed convertibles for its home market, started to build convertibles for export (SAAB's 900 cabriolet arrived in the mid-1980s and Volvo's 480ES cabriolet a few years later).

Many of the world's most attractive and desirable cars have been convertibles, and the decline in the number of open cars available during the 1970s made that decade a dreary one for motoring enthusiasts. At long last, after a further decade of indecision, the convertible seems to be making a comeback. Time alone will tell whether the convertibles of the future will live up to the standards set by so many of those illustrated in this book.

Top: The Cadillac Allanté was an attempt by America's premier luxury-car manufacturer to break into the two-seater market. It was not as successful as its makers had hoped. This is a 1990 model.

Above: Japanese manufacturers were late in getting into the market for sporting convertibles, but when they did they produced some remarkable designs, such as this 2-liter Toyota Celica dating from 1988.

Right: During the 1980s, four-wheel-drive vehicles made inroads into the 'fun-car' market. Among them were convertible versions, such as this Suzuki Vitara – in fact, a 1992 model.

THE CONVERTIBLE SINCE 1945

22 CLASSIC CONVERTIBLES

When World War II ended, the British car industry encountered very different trading conditions from those which it had enjoyed in the 1930s. In the harsher climate of the late 1940s it found that it could no longer build solely for its home market and for a captive and protected market in the British Commonwealth. Instead, it was obliged to compete head-to-head with foreign manufacturers for new export markets, in order to earn the revenue to rebuild Britain's war-torn economy. Inevitably, these new conditions had their effect on the cars which came from Britain.

Even so, it took several years for the traditional British way of doing things to die out. One reason for this was that the austere British roadster (as exemplified by the MG T-series) found a ready market in the United States, and it was not until the late 1950s that the American preference for such creature comforts as winding windows, leak-proof soft tops, and heaters which worked, fundamentally changed the British two-seater.

Britain also continued to build 1930s-style tourers until well into the 1950s. There were two main reasons for their demise: the first being dwindling sales and the second being associated with the practicalities of their manufacture. In the first half of the 1950s there were still many cars – mainly the more expensive types – which had separate-chassis construction, and for these the great British coachbuilders could construct open bodywork relatively easily. However, the mass manufacturers were increasingly turning to unitary construction. This was much more difficult to use as the basis of open bodywork, not least because removing a stressed roof panel left the rest of the bodyshell in need of careful and potentially very expensive structural reinforcement. The coachbuilders, in the main, were not prepared to undertake this kind of work, which was outside the scope of their traditional skills.

As a result, the mass manufacturers increasingly engineered and built their own open versions of unitary-construction cars. Or, when the costs would have been too high, they simply deleted such models from their ranges. Short of work, the traditional coachbuilders closed down one by one, or were bought out by the car manufacturers themselves. The majority had suffered one or other of these fates by the end of the 1950s, and the last major independent coachbuilder – James Young – closed in 1967. Long before then, however, its customers had been reduced to just two: Rolls-Royce and Bentley.

There have been three major types of British convertible since 1945. The smallest (in terms of passenger space, at least) are the sports convertibles,

Preceding pages: The epitomy of the elegant British drophead coupe of the 1950s – the 1954 Alvis TC21/100.

Below left: This Daimler DB18 is typical of the upper-crust British convertible of the 1940s.

Right: The Austin Atlantic shows what happened when British stylists tried to appeal to the American market.

Center right: This 1951 Lagonda 2.5-liter drophead coupe added flowing fender lines to upright styling.

Below right: Triumph's bulbous-looking 1800 roadster – actually a 1940s drophead coupe.

These pages: The variety of British convertibles available in the 1950s is well illustrated by this selection. The Ford Zodiac at top left was the most expensive of Ford's British products, but the 1956 Bentley S-type, with its coachbuilt body by Park Ward, at bottom left cost well over five times as much. The 1955 Sunbeam Mark III (top right) looked rather stodgy, although related models notched up sporting successes. However, for a true sports convertible there was little to better the Jaguar XK120 (below), seen here in rare drophead-coupe guise.

Left: The 1964 Aston Martin DB5 drophead coupe had a 282bhp, 3995cc straight-six engine which propelled it to 140mph. Even greater performance was available with the later 314bhp Vantage engine option.

Above right: The Ford Zephyr 6 of the late 1950s was slightly less expensive than the Zodiac illustrated on page 24. Most of the differences were cosmetic or in equipment levels, but both cars had a power-operated convertible top.

Below right: The original styling by the Swiss coachbuilder Graber for Alvis dated from the mid-1950s. By 1965, when this elegant TE21 3-liter drophead was built, only minor revisions had been made.

essentially civilized descendants of the traditional open roadster. Above them are those cars based on family sedans which, until the end of the 1960s, were the inheritors of the old tourer tradition, but which have recently had both a more youthful appeal and a more overtly sporting flavor. Then right at the top of the tree are the expensive coachbuilt luxury convertibles, of which some have sporting pretensions while others are closer to the tourer tradition.

The Sports Convertible

Jaguar was offering both sidescreen-roadster and sports-convertible versions of its XK120 model as early as 1948, but its example was not generally followed until the end of the 1950s and the beginning of the 1960s. During this period the traditionally austere British roadster was almost universally replaced by the sports convertible. These cars did not look radically different from their predecessors, but the changes were there nonetheless. The new breed was exemplified in 1961 by the Jaguar E-type and Triumph TR4, in 1962 by the Triumph Spitfire, MGB and Austin-Healey 3000 Mark II; from 1964 the cheaper models, in the shape of the Austin-Healey Sprite and MG Midget, also gained winding windows. From then on few two-seater sports-cars built in Britain retained the old style of sidescreens and frugal interior appointments, and those which did – such as the Morgan and the Lotus 7 – were sold only in limited numbers and were widely considered among non-enthusiasts to be eccentric throwbacks.

The major British manufacturers had become heavily dependent upon sales in the United States and, when it began to look as if new safety legislation in America would ban the sale of open cars in that market altogether during the 1970s, they stopped developing new sports convertibles. Old designs were allowed to die out and were not replaced, although the open MGB, MG Midget and Triumph Spitfire remained in production right through

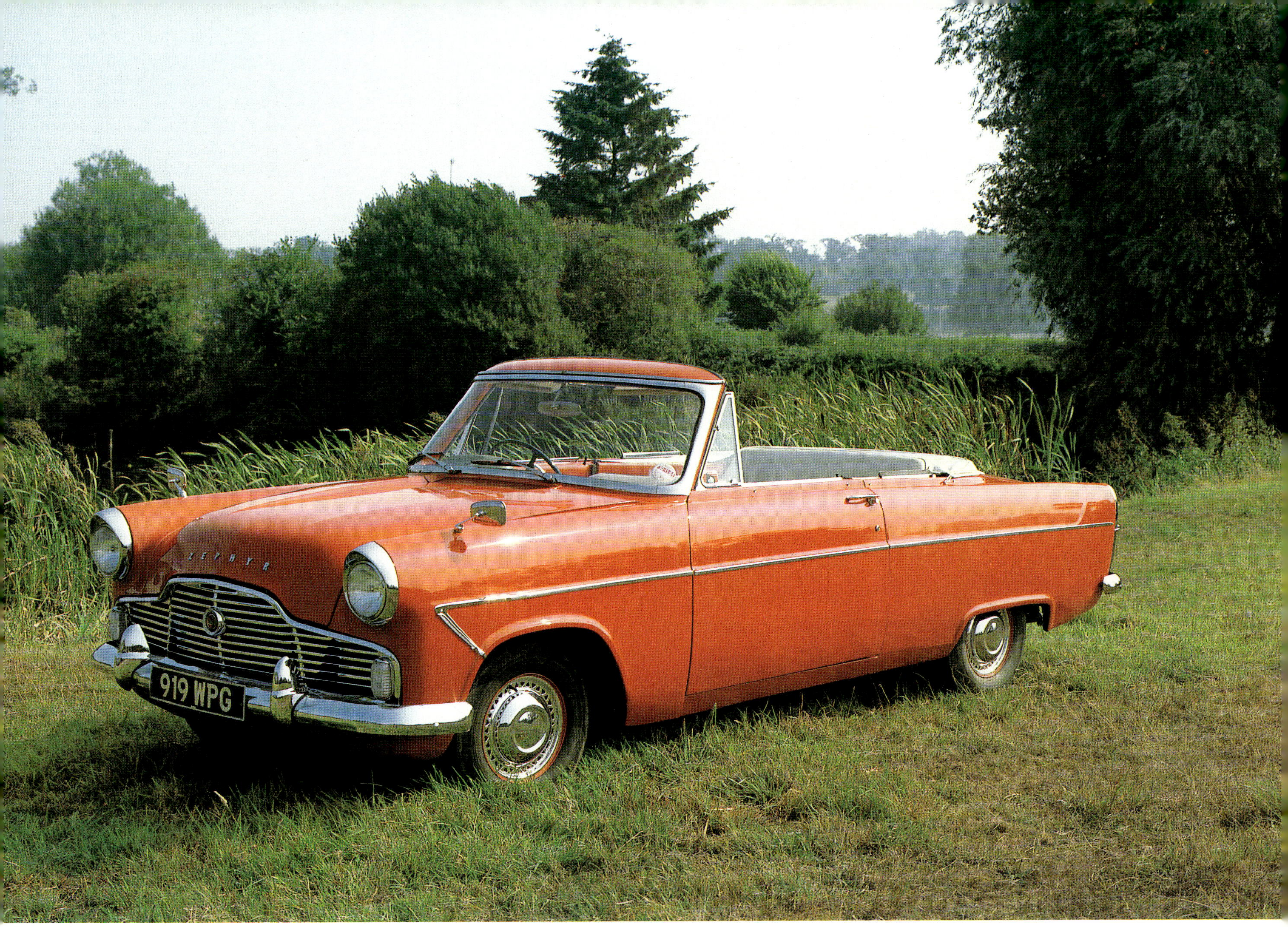
919 WPG

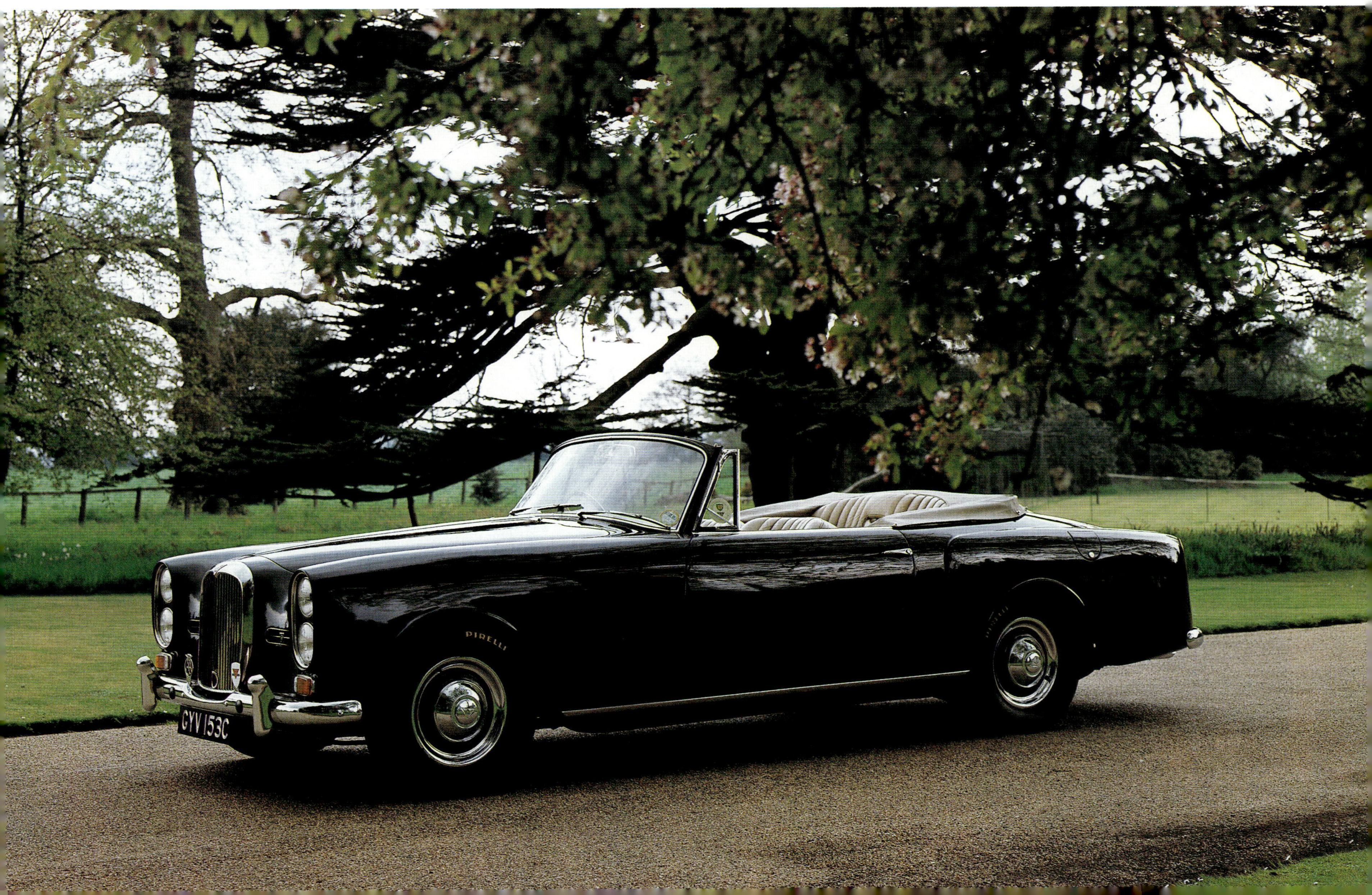
GYV 153C

28 CLASSIC CONVERTIBLES

the 1970s. By the end of the decade it was clear that the anticipated new legislation would not be introduced, and new sports convertibles therefore began to appear. Triumph redeveloped its fixed-head TR7 into an attractive open model, but the market for such cars had shrunk considerably, and the TR7 convertible lasted only until 1981.

Today the market for sports convertibles is still uncertain, and the major British manufacturers have fought shy of committing themselves to it. Small manufacturers like Reliant, Marcos and Panther are still making such cars, but a brave attempt by Lotus with the Elan SE in 1989 quickly foundered. The Rover Group, which now owns the traditional names of Triumph, Austin-Healey and MG, introduced an updated, limited-edition revival of the MGB in 1992, and there are rumors that a full-production open two-seater is on the way. As for Jaguar, it has deserted the two-seater market for the more lucrative one of the luxury convertible.

These pages: In the sportscar field, Triumph's TR range was among Britain's proudest exports. On the left is a 1967 TR4A model with a Surrey top; bottom right is a 1972 TR6, the last separate-chassis TR model; and at top right is a sleek 1979 TR7 drophead. Triumph's major competition among domestic manufacturers came from MG, whose MGB (top left) was introduced in 1961 and remained in production for 20 years. However, none of these sportscars offered four proper seats; for that, the family buyer of an open car in Britain had to think of something considerably less sporting, like the much-loved 1-liter Morris Minor, seen at bottom left in 1967 tourer guise.

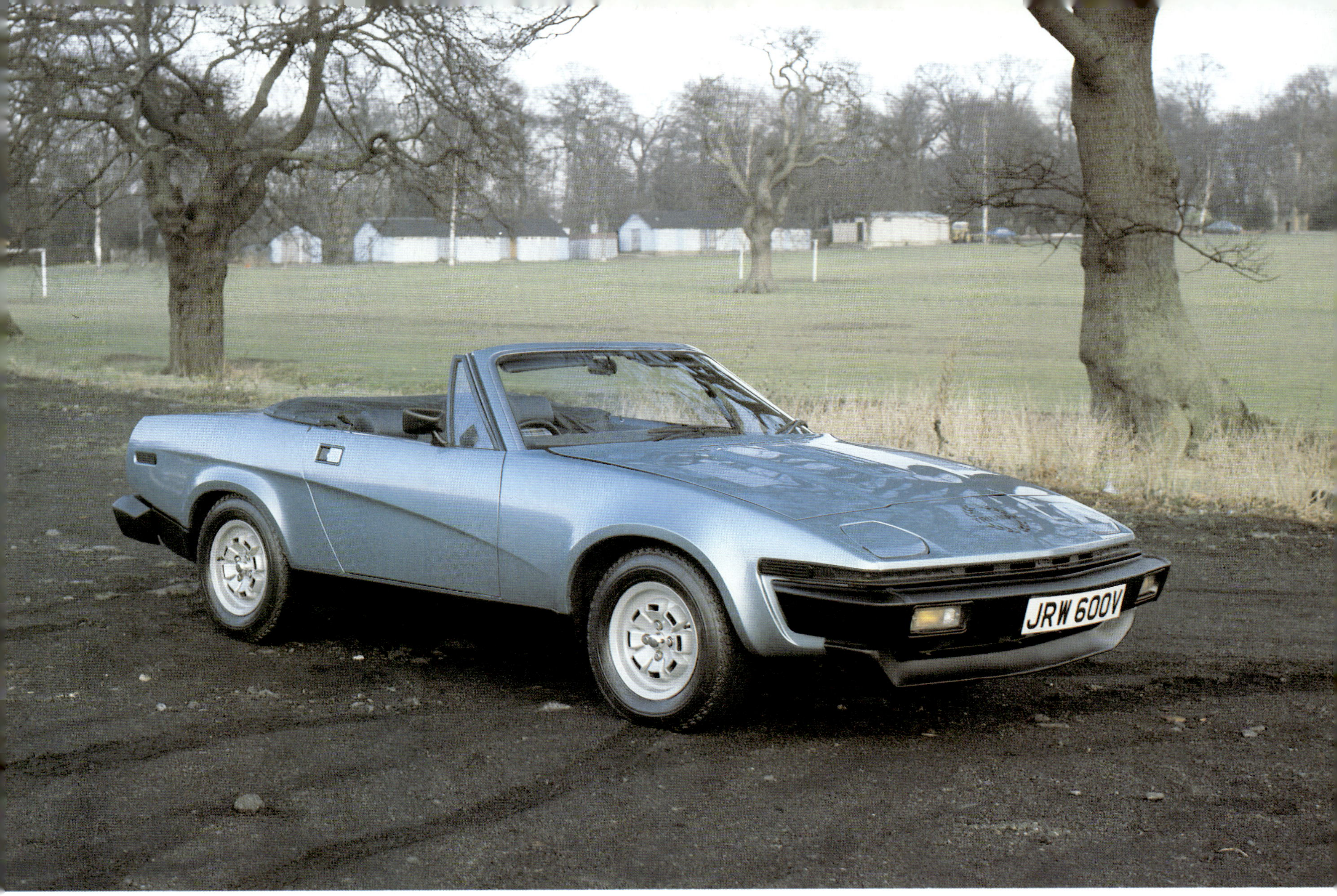
JRW 600V

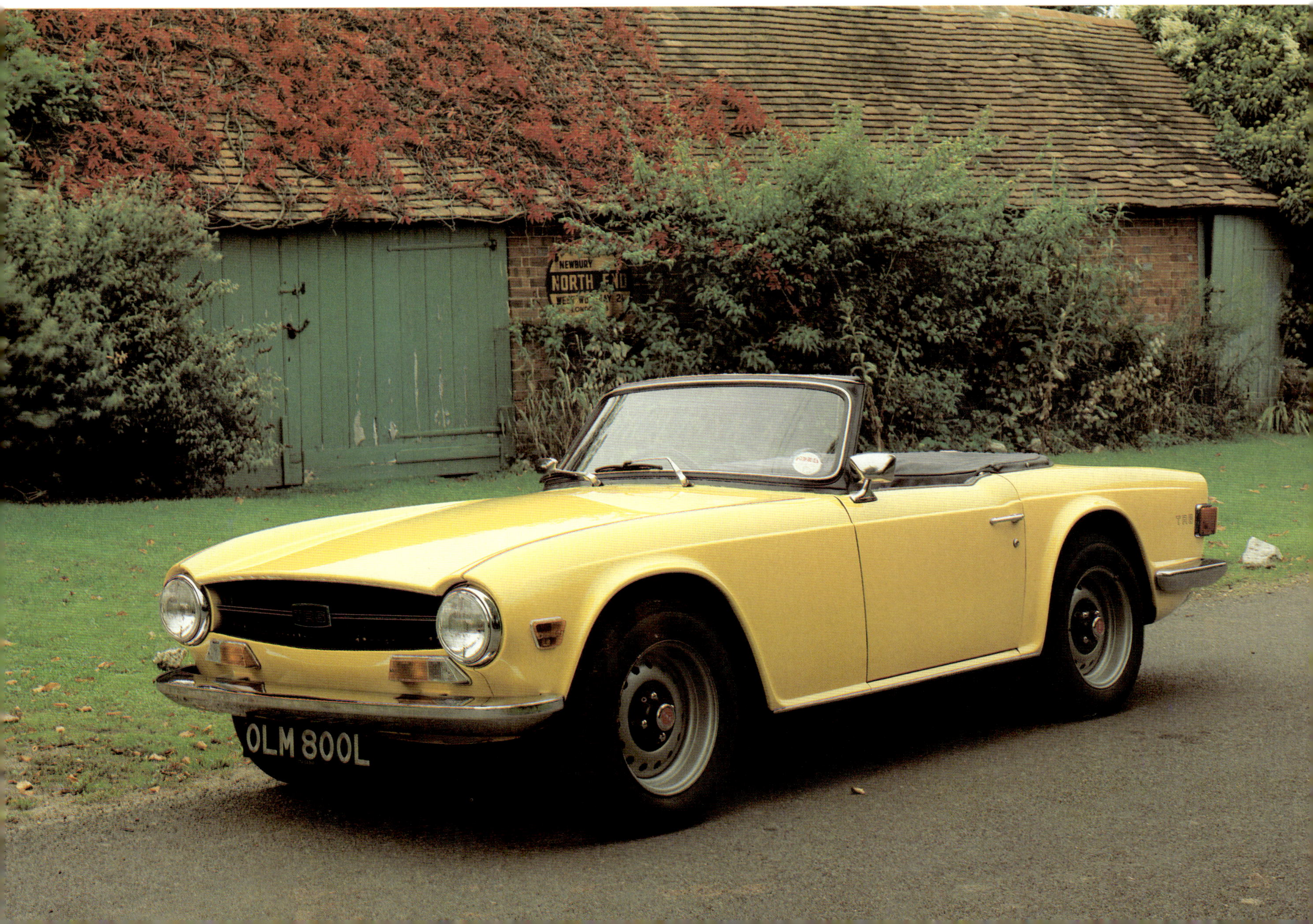
NORTH END
OLM 800L

These pages: Britain was always noted for its affordable sportscars, like the remarkable backbone-chassis, GRP-bodied Lotus Elan (left), seen here in 1968-onwards Series 4 guise. In the high-performance luxury market, Jensen offered the Interceptor convertible, seen below as a 1974 Series III model. Even more expensive was the Rolls-Royce Corniche (right), introduced in 1971 but based on a mid-1960s design. And among the immortals was the Jaguar E-type (bottom right), which sported a 5.3-liter V12 engine by the time this 1973 example was built.

These pages: Like many other manufacturers, Jaguar played for safety when reintroducing open models in the 1980s. Before the fully-open version of the XJ-S could appear in 1988 (top left), a Targa-top 'cabriolet' (bottom right) was available for five years. Cheap sportscars like the Triumph Spitfire (left) remained on sale throughout the 1970s, but no new models were developed to replace them because of fears about legislation. When those fears had been laid to rest and confidence started to return to the open-car market, smaller manufacturers like TVR introduced open models. Top right is a TVR 350i of the mid-1980s.

The Tourer and its Descendants

The second major type of British convertible is that based on a middle-class family sedan. At the cheaper end of this market the volume manufacturers always built their own bodywork, which generally closely resembled that of the sedan on which the car was based. In the late 1940s MG based its YT tourer on the YA sedan, while Morris developed its Minor tourer from the Minor sedan in 1948 and continued building versions of it for the next 21 years. The Rootes Group served British customers well for a decade and a half, beginning with a drophead-coupe version of its Sunbeam-Talbot 90 in 1948, and working through successive varieties of the Hillman Minx and its closely-related sisters, the Sunbeam Rapier and Singer Gazelle. Ford, perhaps surprisingly, came up with some delightful convertibles based on its Consul and Zephyr sedan ranges in the 1950s and early 1960s.

Farther up the market, AC, Alvis and Armstrong Siddeley started out well in the late 1940s, but their traditional tourers were appealing to dwindling numbers of customers and, by the mid-1950s, all of these companies had turned elsewhere for inspiration. Alvis went farther up-market toward the end of the decade with the TD21 convertible, styled by the Swiss coachbuilder Graber, but found itself out on a limb and ceased production in 1967. Daimler was unable to sell its delicious coachbuilt models beyond the middle of the 1950s, and Riley gave up on its 2.5-liter drophead coupe in 1951 after just three years of slow production.

The more expensive middle-class convertibles were largely extinct by the middle of the 1950s; the mass-market types lingered on for another decade or so, but they too were dead by the end of the 1960s. Sales volumes had not been high enough to justify developing convertible versions of the new sedans planned for the 1970s – and besides, the fear that other countries

Above: Still at the pinnacle of the luxury-convertible market is the Rolls-Royce Corniche, which has been gradually and subtly updated since its introduction 20 years before this 1992-model Corniche IV Anniversary Edition was built.

Left: The convertible returned to the family-car market in the 1980s, with cars like the Ford Escort cabriolet. Although generally perceived as a British car in Britain, this 1989 model was actually built in Germany.

Top right: Another British family convertible which isn't: the Rover 214 of 1992 is heavily based on a Japanese Honda sedan, although the styling and (in this case) the engine are British.

Right: British through and through, except that the body was designed in Italy! This is a 1990 example of the limited-edition Aston Martin Zagato, an exclusive and costly convertible supercar.

might follow the widely-expected American legislation banning open cars of all kinds made it commercially risky to build such cars. Conversion specialists like Crayford Engineering did build convertible versions of family sedans during the 1970s, as they had in the previous decade, but their products were only available in tiny numbers. During the 1980s the British sedan-based convertible appeared to make a comeback in the shape of the Ford Escort cabriolet and the much rarer Vauxhall Cavalier convertible, but in truth both cars were built in Germany.

It was the beginning of the 1990s before things began to look up again in this sector of the market. Following the success of foreign manufacturers' sedan-based convertibles, Rover announced three new convertible models in 1992. The smallest of these was the Mini convertible, based on the long-running Mini introduced in 1959; next up was a convertible based on the Metro hatchback first seen in 1980; and lastly came a particularly attractive convertible version of the successful 200-series sedan, introduced in 1989.

The Luxury Convertible

The third and most expensive type of British convertible is the luxury convertible, distinguished by its quality of materials and level of appointments, and typified by Rolls-Royce and Bentley models. However, these two major names are by no means the only representatives. Lagonda and Daimler made convertibles for this market in the late 1940s and early 1950s, and even the Rootes Group — better known for its mass-market models — tried hard to compete in 1949-50, with a convertible Humber Super Snipe whose bodywork was by the coachbuilders Tickford.

Other manufacturers in this sector of the market have included Bristol (from the late 1940s to the present), Jensen (from 1950), and Aston Martin, the latter building cars with a distinctive sporting flavor as well as all the traditional hallmarks of the coachbuilt British convertible. Yet such cars, by virtue of their cost, have been, and continue to be, built in small numbers. Perhaps the most successful company in recent years has been Jaguar, which announced Targa-type convertible versions of its XJ-S grand tourer in 1983 and full convertible versions in 1988.

The German Convertible

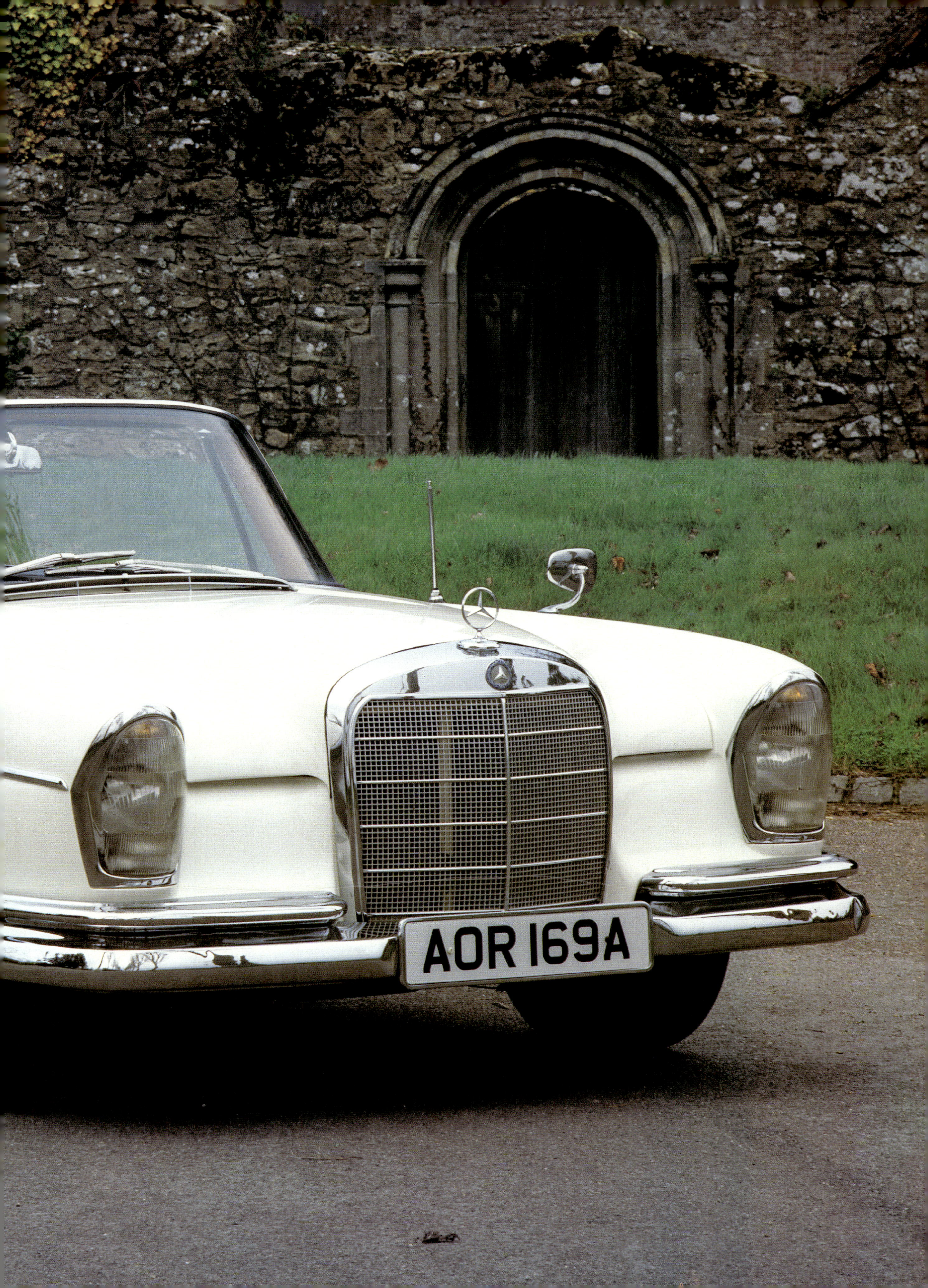
AOR 169A

38 CLASSIC CONVERTIBLES

Germany emerged from World War II with her motor industry in ruins. Many factories had been bombed to rubble in Allied air raids, and the division of the country into Eastern and Western sectors had severed connections between suppliers and manufacturers and, in many cases, had left parts of the same company separated by a border which, in due course, became known as the Iron Curtain. As the country began to recover, it became clear that it would be the Western sector which would continue the great traditions of Germany's prewar motor industry; in the Eastern sector communist policies tied the hands of motor manufacturers, and East Germany's motor industry became largely irrelevant in world terms.

In 1945 West Germany was in urgent need of vehicles of all kinds, for without them it had no chance of rebuilding its economy. As there was no money with which to import such vehicles, the only option was to make them at home. In those austere times, such frivolities as open cars were frowned upon, and the first years of postwar motor production in Germany were devoted largely to commercial vehicles and mundane sedan cars.

However, things soon began to improve. In 1948 came complete monetary reform and the first installments of a massive injection of economic aid from the USA. In the motor industry the results were apparent almost immediately, and the first postwar convertibles appeared in 1948-49 from Volkswagen, Mercedes-Benz and Borgward. As the industry gathered strength, so the production of more and more convertibles was announced, and the 1950s saw a rapid expansion of the numbers and types available.

Much as in Britain, Germany produced three major types of convertible

Previous pages: This 1963 Mercedes-Benz 220SE typifies all that is best about the sedan-based convertibles from Germany.

Top left: BMW's 503 convertible was a luxury model which failed to make a significant impact on the market, despite its undoubted excellence.

Left: The primary aim of the Porsche 356 cabriolet was to combine open-air motoring with sporting performance and handling. This 1951 example had its VW-derived air-cooled engine mounted at the rear.

Above: When Mercedes-Benz entered the two-seater sportscar market with the 190SL in 1954, its product was typically German: refined, heavy, durable and beautifully built and engineered.

Right: This picture of a 1957 300SL Mercedes-Benz clearly shows its family resemblance to the cheaper 190SL. The difference was more marked on the open road: the 300SL was capable of 125mph or more (depending on specification), while the 190SL peaked at around 105mph.

40 CLASSIC CONVERTIBLES

These pages: Three very different approaches to the sedan-based convertible: top left is the Karmann convertible version of Volkswagen's best-selling Beetle sedan; top right is a convertible version of the Messerschmitt Tiger bubble-car, which was produced in the late 1950s for the economy-car market; and on the right is a 220SE Mercedes-Benz cabriolet dating from 1960, with a fuel-injected 2.2-liter engine which gave a top speed of well over 100mph.

THE GERMAN CONVERTIBLE

car. The first to reappear after the war were the cheapest and easiest to produce – the sedan-based convertibles – and this type still exists today, although it has evolved to meet changing tastes. The large luxury convertible returned in the early 1950s as the German economy began to stabilize and flourish, but the market for such cars was inevitably limited and, by the end of the following decade, only one model was still in production. That, too, died out in the early 1970s and was not replaced.

The sports convertible also proliferated in the 1950s as the German 'economic miracle' produced conditions in which there was room for such cars alongside rather more practical means of transport. German sports convertibles were almost always better equipped than their contemporaries from other European countries, and they were also much more expensive. Accidents of design, rather than careful planning, enabled the open sports models of Porsche and Mercedes-Benz to survive the 1970s, with their uncertainties about the future of open cars, and new designs began to appear once again in the 1980s.

Sedan-based Convertibles

The first sedan-based convertibles to appear were, in fact, factory-approved conversions of the Volkswagen Beetle – a two-seater by Hebmüller in 1948, and a four-seater by Karmann in 1949 – but it was not long before the manufacturers of larger and more expensive cars also risked new open models. Hebmüller again was responsible for the 1949 convertible version of Borgward's slab-sided 1.5-liter 1500 sedan, but Mercedes-Benz constructed the bodies for its 170S cabriolets in-house. There were two types of 170S cabriolet – a sporting Cabriolet A, and a roomier Cabriolet B – but the most important pointer for the future was that they were based on the car which was then

CLASSIC CONVERTIBLES

Mercedes-Benz's most expensive model, rather than on the humbler 170V sedan. The Stuttgart company would always aim higher than the market for which Volkswagen catered.

Throughout the 1950s, Volkswagen was pre-eminent in this market, supplementing its Beetle-based cabriolet with a pretty Karmann-Ghia model in 1957 and thus gathering welcome extra sales. DKW also offered cheap convertible versions of its two-stroke sedans from the early 1950s, and their successors remained available under the Auto Union name, and with pseudo-American styling by Baur, until 1965. One rung farther up the ladder, Borgward attempted to satisfy the customers which Mercedes-Benz had deserted when it moved up-market, but its 1952 1800 convertible and the considerably more attractive Isabella replacement of 1955 remained rare and made little impact outside Germany.

Borgward went under in 1961, the year in which BMW tackled the small-cabriolet market with a convertible version of its 700, a rear-engined economy car with attractive styling by the Italian Michelotti. Success was limited: BMW did much better with its more expensive 1600 cabriolet (1967) and Targa-top 3-series cars of the 1970s, and with the full convertibles on the second-generation 3-series models in the mid-1980s.

By the later 1970s, the sporting hatchback was largely replacing the open sportscar as a fun car for younger drivers, and Volkswagen was the first to address the demand for convertible versions of such cars, with its Karmann-built Golf cabriolet of 1979. Other German manufacturers took some time to catch up, and indeed Ford had no convertible Escort until 1984, while Opel did not introduce open Kadetts (by Bertone in Italy) and Asconas (by Baur) until the mid-1980s.

Above left: BMW employed the Italian Michelotti to style its small, rear-engined 700 model, of which this convertible is a 1961 example.

Above right: There could be little doubt that the American Ford Thunderbird had inspired the styling of Auto Union's 1958 1000SP. The power train was rather different, however: instead of the Ford's big V8, the Auto Union had a 55bhp three-cylinder engine!

Left: The 1969 Targa-top Porsche 914 was the result of a collaboration between Volkswagen and Porsche. However, its appeal remained limited.

Top right: The open version of the Volkswagen Karmann Ghia 1500 was an attractive-looking car, but without the performance to match those looks. The design dated from the 1950s, but this is a 1968 model.

Right: With this Targa-top version of its 911 sports model, Porsche was sure it could continue to sell cars if open models were outlawed in the USA in the later 1970s. This is a 1975 example.

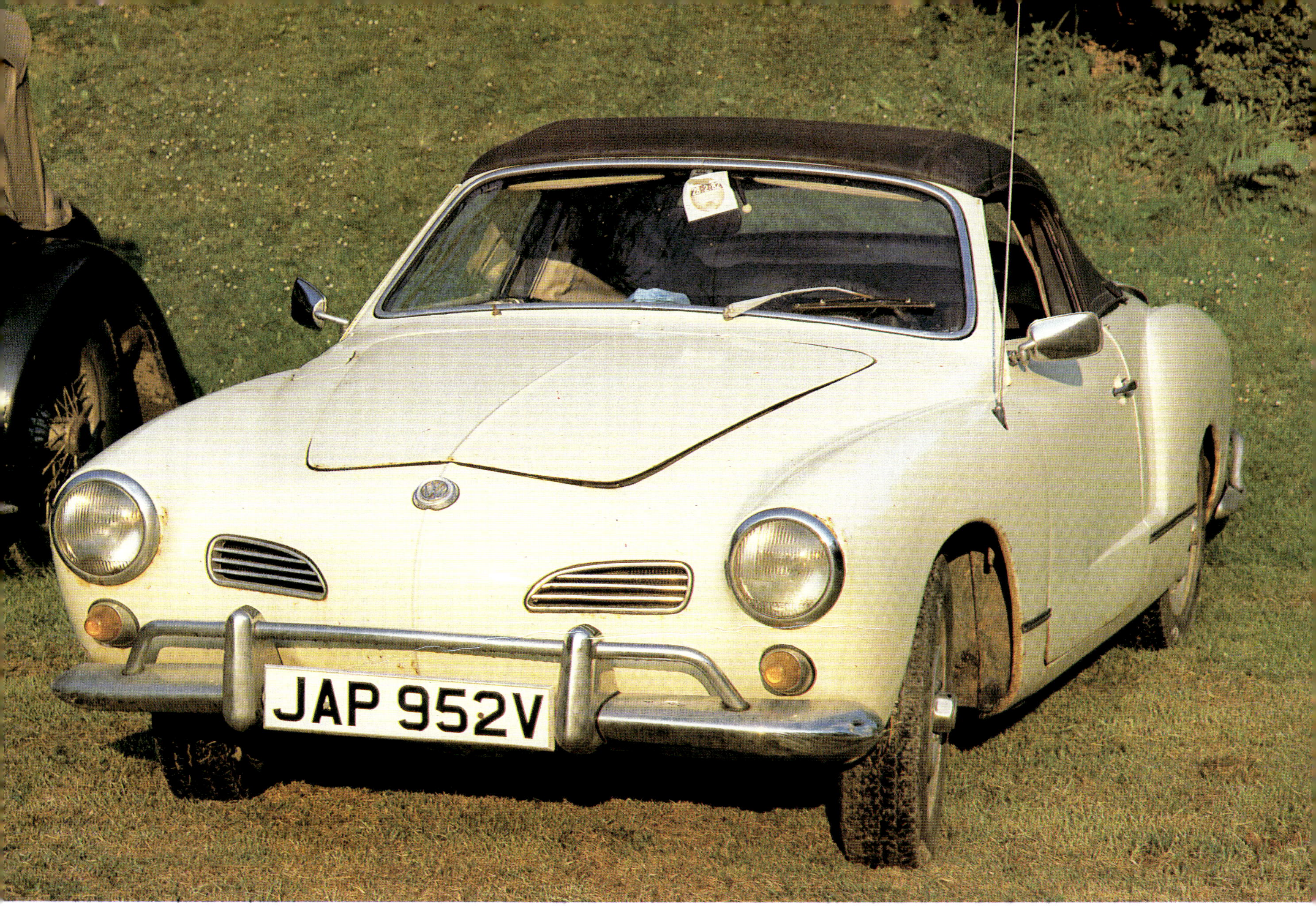
JAP 952V

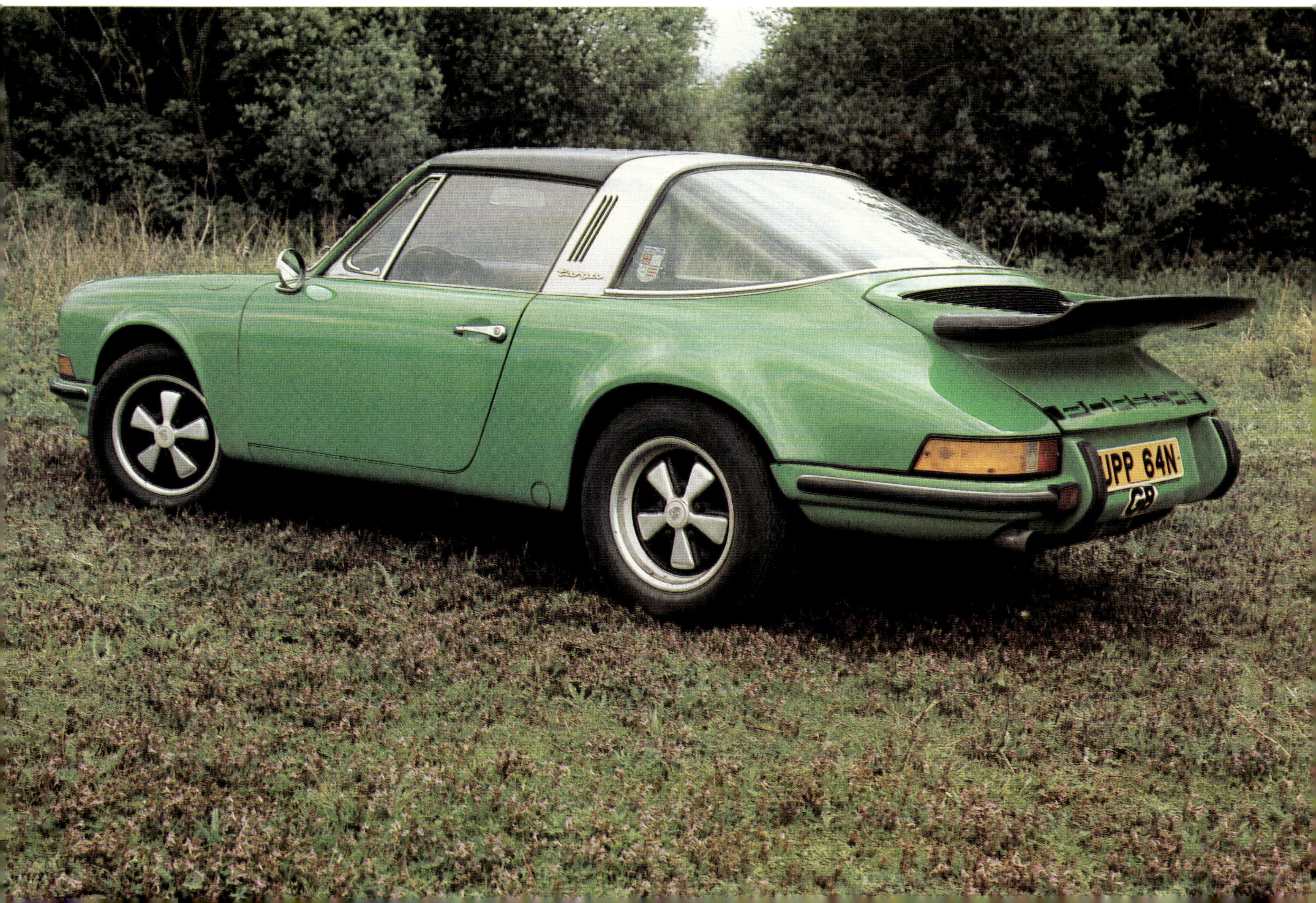
UPP 64N

44 CLASSIC CONVERTIBLES

Meanwhile, Mercedes-Benz had moved its convertibles into a completely different market. The Mercedes-Benz convertibles were always based on the most expensive of the company's medium-sized sedans, and before long their styling made the cars' sedan origins less apparent and added a cachet of exclusivity. The 170S lasted only two years; it was replaced in 1951 by a 220S, which in turn gave way to a new-model 220S in 1955. By the time of 1961's 220SE and the related 300SE of 1962, Mercedes-Benz cars had moved into the luxury-convertible market.

Luxury Convertibles

The luxury convertible returned to Germany later than the sedan-based open cars, for the simple reason that the German economy would not have supported such a product earlier. Mercedes-Benz judged that the time was right to introduce a luxury model in 1951, and that year announced the production of three open cars related to its new 300 3-liter prestige sedan. These were the 300S roadster (nowhere near as austere as its name suggests) and 300S cabriolet, both on a short-wheelbase chassis, and a full-sized 300 Cabriolet D, which was a four-door open version of the sedan. However, the market for expensive cars like these did not last. The 300S models disappeared in 1958 and the 300 Cabriolet D was withdrawn from the market in 1962.

As far as Mercedes-Benz was concerned, the new cabriolets based on its medium-sized sedans were an adequate replacement. The top-model 300SE was its representative in this segment of the market in the early 1960s, but as the related 220SE turned first into a 250SE and then a 280SE, the gap between the expensive middle-class car and the top, luxury model became narrower. From 1969, the two fused in the 280SE 3.5, a V8-engined model which lasted until 1971. Like other manufacturers, Mercedes-Benz avoided developing new convertibles in the 1970s, and in fact did not return to the luxury-convertible market until 1992, with a cabriolet version of its 300CE-24 coupe.

In the luxury-convertible sector, Mercedes-Benz's only real competitor on the home market was BMW, which introduced its six-cylinder 501 convertible (by Baur) in 1954, and continued to offer similar vehicles — latterly based on the V8-engined 502 — until 1963. The company's attempt to rival the Mercedes-Benz 300S with the 503 of 1955 foundered in 1959, however, after only a few hundred had been built: the market was simply not big enough, as Mercedes-Benz had also found.

Left: Volkswagen's convertible version of its trend-setting GTi hatchback led the way for other makers. The car offered four-seat accommodation as well as a sparkling performance from its fuel-injected 1588cc four-cylinder engine, and was widely seen as a practical modern equivalent of the two-seater sportscar. The extra weight of the Karmann-converted body made it slightly slower than the sedan version of the GTi. This 1988 example still looked very much like the original open Golf, first announced in 1979.

Right: BMW's 3-series sedans were one of the success stories of the 1970s and 1980s, and open versions appeared in the late 1970s. Like many other manufacturers, however, BMW proceeded with caution: the first open 3-series cars were Targa-top 'cabriolets' converted by Baur, and full convertibles did not appear until much later. This is a 1984 320i Targa-top, with a 125bhp fuel-injected 2-liter engine.

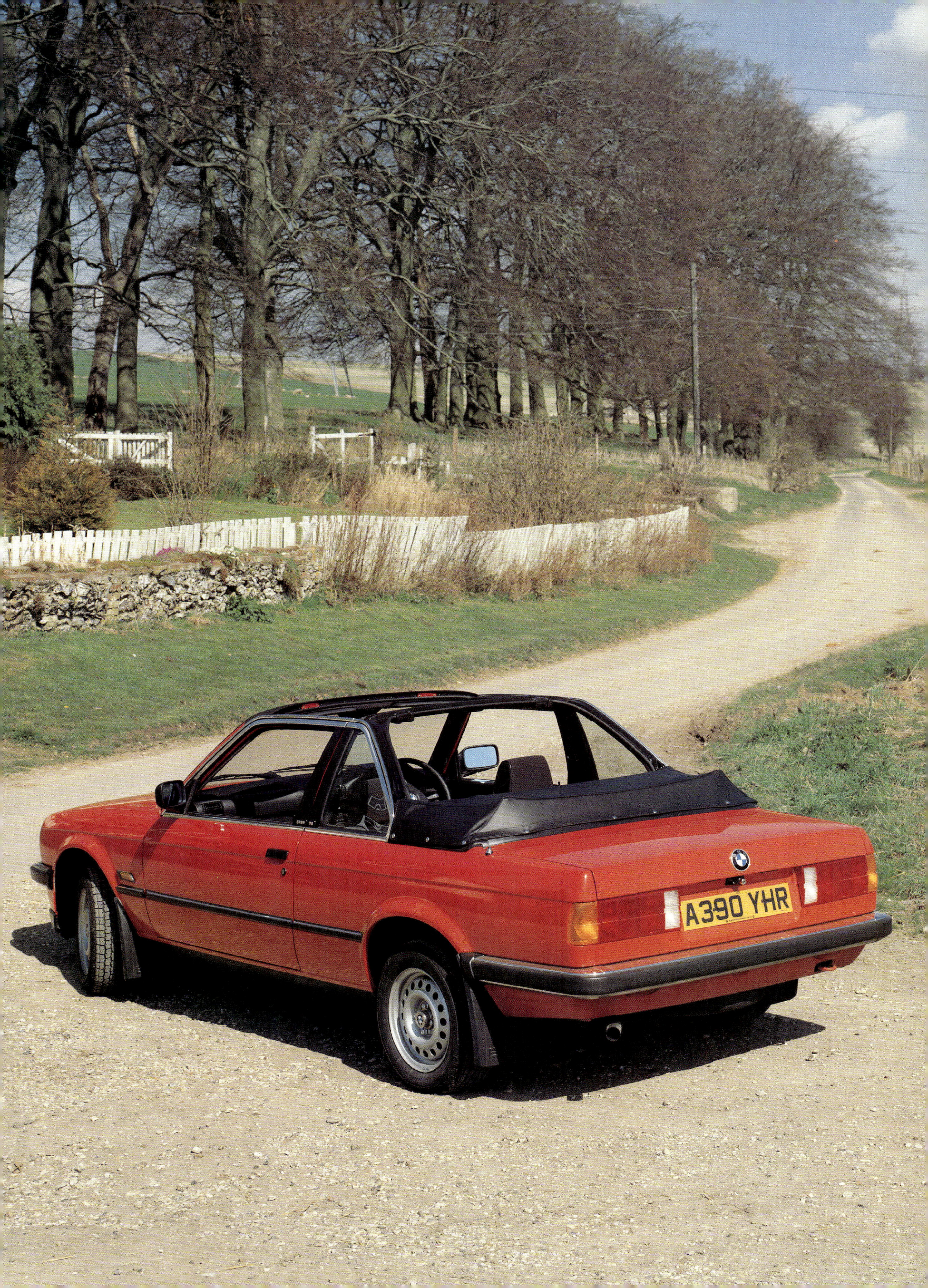
A390 YHR

Above: The BMW Z1 of 1989 was designed around the 170bhp 2.5-liter six-cylinder engine of the 325i sedan. Its cost put it beyond the reach of most two-seater sportscar buyers, but for the lucky few who could afford one, the rewards were exciting performance and superb handling.

Above right: Audi's four-wheel-drive five-cylinder Quattro of 1980 came only as a coupe, but German conversion specialist Walter Treser offered a convertible version later in the decade. Only small numbers were built.

Right: The fully-open 3-series BMW appeared in 1986. Various sizes of engine were available, and this 1989 car is fitted with the 2.5-liter fuel-injected six-cylinder, which combined refinement with real punch.

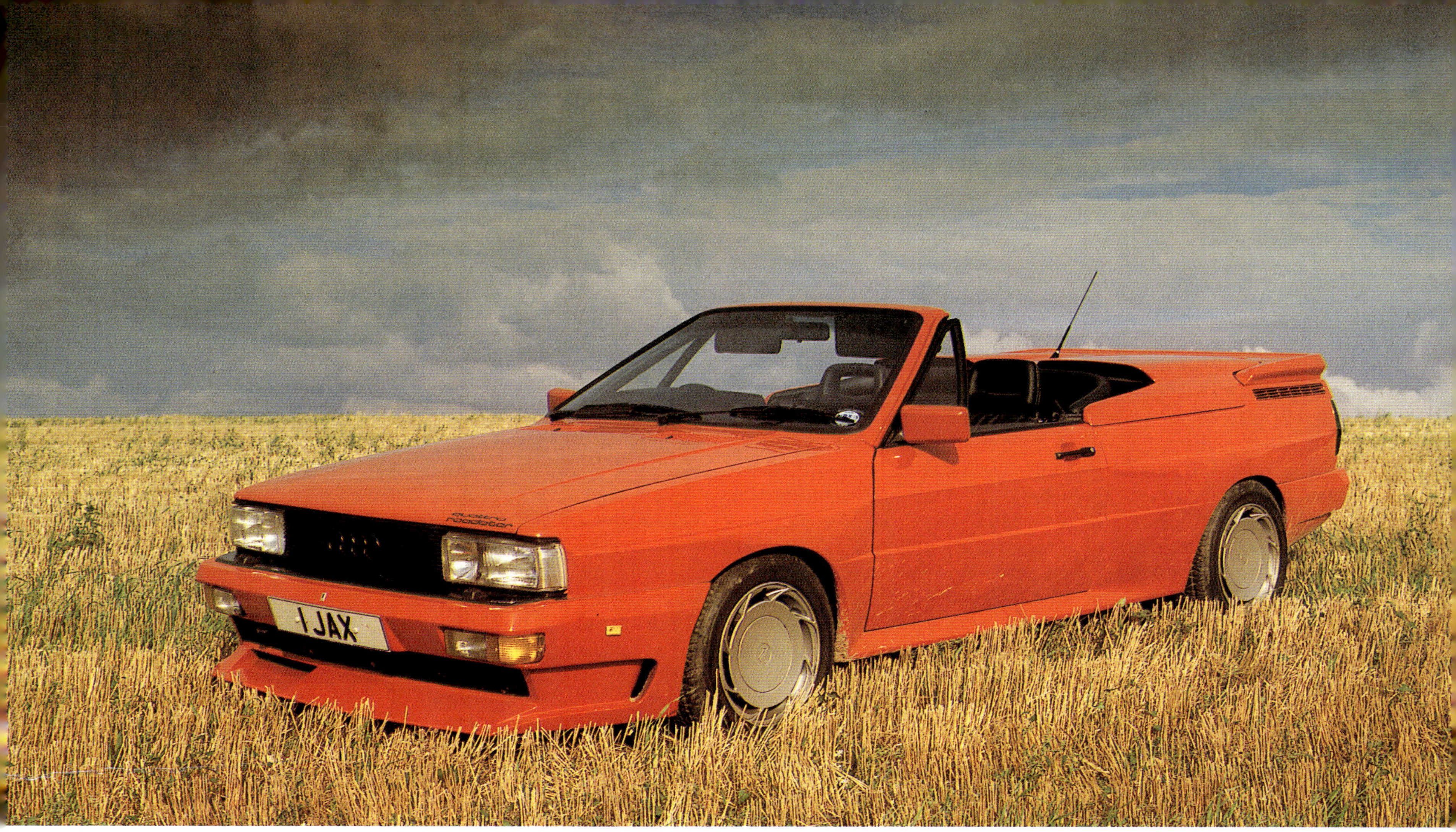
1 JAX

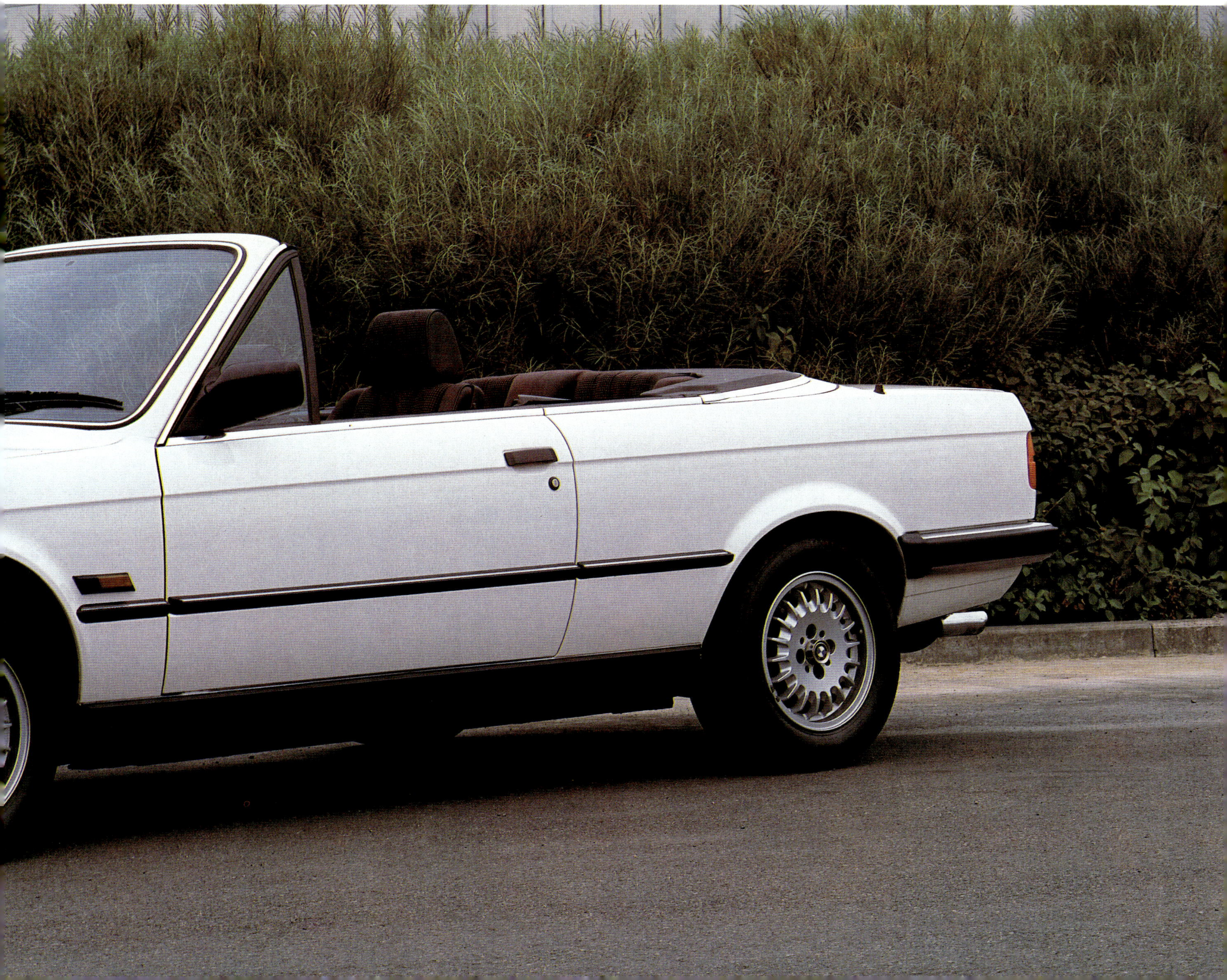

48 CLASSIC CONVERTIBLES

Sports Convertibles

Although the open sportscar did not become established in Germany again until after the luxury convertible had made its reappearance, it did, in fact, arrive slightly earlier. The brave entrant into an uncertain market in 1950 was the new Porsche company, which announced the production of open versions of its Volkswagen-derived 356 sports coupe. These remained available until production of the 356 ended in the early 1960s.

In the sportscar field, it was Porsche which became, and has remained, the leading German manufacturer. The open 356 was not directly replaced but, after a gap of some four years, Porsche introduced a Targa-top version of its 911 coupe. This satisfied demand throughout the 1970s, a period when the future of the fully-open sportscar looked doubtful; and, in 1982, as confidence began to return to the market, a 911 cabriolet was announced.

Porsche's cars were always expensive and exclusive, and in 1969 the company attempted to break into a lower price bracket through a link-up with Volkswagen. The resulting Targa-topped 914 was an intriguing hybrid, but was nevertheless too expensive to meet its manufacturers' sales targets. Production stopped after just four years, after which Porsche returned to the market it knew best. Subsequent convertibles were based on its existing coupes: the 911 in 1982, the 944S in 1988, and the 968 in 1991.

Mercedes-Benz and BMW also tackled the open sportscar market, although BMW's only serious entry was the 507, built between 1956 and 1959 and unable to compete with the Stuttgart products. Its 1988 Z1 was always intended to be a limited-volume model, produced to test the market for possible future products. Mercedes-Benz started with the 190SL in 1954, which was followed in 1957 by a luxurious open 'roadster' version of the 300SL gull-wing coupe – one of the supercars of the era. The Mercedes-Benz tradition was well established by 1963 when the new 230SL arrived, and this in turn was upgraded over the years, being replaced in 1971 by a 350SL and subsequent derivatives. The latest models, introduced in 1989 and centering on the 500SL, carry on the Mercedes-Benz 'SL' tradition of costly open two-seaters, with high levels of equipment, comfort, performance and roadability. Since 1963 all SLs have been available with detachable hard tops – one reason why Mercedes-Benz continued to build them throughout the 1970s in apparent defiance of the threatened US legislation against open cars.

These pages: Porsche adapted swiftly to a market in which open cars were making a comeback during the 1980s. By the end of the decade it had open versions of its evergreen 911 (left) and 944 (above). At the end of 1991, the 944 was replaced by the 968 (above, left), of which an open version was also available. The basic 911 design dated back to the early 1960s but, by the time of the 1992 model pictured, it had undergone considerable development and was still among the most sought-after prestige sportscars. Whereas the 911's engine was rear-mounted, the 944 — pictured in 1990 944S2 guise — and 968 both had front-mounted engines. All were highly desirable pieces of property, the main drawback to ownership being their high cost.

The French Convertible

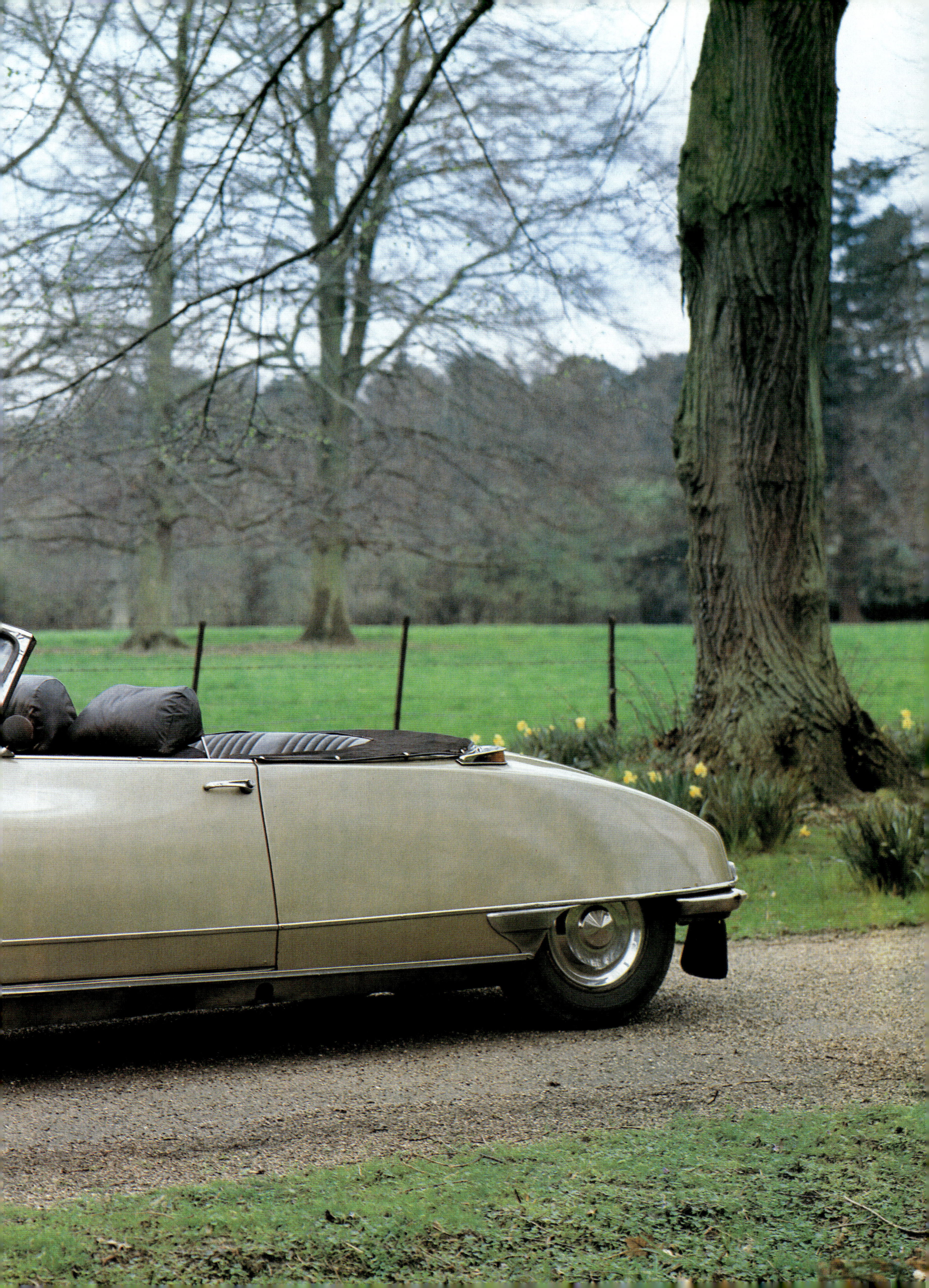

Throughout the period since 1945, French motor manufacturers have been preoccupied with size and, more particularly, with how to minimize it. The reasons for this are not hard to find. After the end of World War II, a new motor-taxation policy added to the existing levy on gasoline: this was a tax based on fiscal horsepower – the French CV rating – which was itself largely dependent on engine capacity. Any engine over about 2.7 liters in capacity was heavily penalized, with the inevitable result that French manufacturers phased out their larger engines. This automatically led to the demise of large cars, at least until advances in engine design allowed smaller-capacity types to provide enough power and torque to haul large and heavy cars around at acceptable speeds.

For the convertible, this new taxation policy was a catastrophe. The traditional French open car of the 1930s had been a *grande routière*, designed to go far and fast across the European continent and endowed with a large-capacity engine and a heavy, coachbuilt body. In postwar France there was no welcome for such cars, and the few manufacturers who tried to build them found the market too restricted to guarantee their survival.

On the other hand, no French manufacturer could deny the value of an open top, whether it was to admit the Mediterranean sunshine or to permit the transporting of oversized loads. Even the 1948 Citroën 2CV economy sedan had a folding roof for such purposes, but the main French manufacturer of 'proper' convertibles right through to the end of the 1970s was Peugeot, which assiduously offered convertible versions of all its major models. Most of Peugeot's convertibles were four-seaters, as were those from the other major manufacturers. Panhard's 1952 Dyna Junior was an exception, but French manufacturers were generally content to leave open sports two-seaters to the British, Germans and Italians.

By the 1980s, however, few French convertibles remained in production. No doubt the threat of American safety legislation banning convertibles, and the likely repercussions of such action worldwide, had inhibited the development of new models in France, just as it had elsewhere. Yet the French convertible did make a comeback in the 1980s, drawing on Volkswagen's Golf-based convertible for its inspiration. By the early 1990s the sporty convertible based on a small family sedan appeared to be gaining some ground in France.

The Last of the Exotics

France's new postwar motor-taxation policies left the manufacturers of the great tourers of the 1930s high and dry, competing with one another for survival in a rapidly shrinking market. Bugatti was already in decline, and was never really a serious car maker after the death of its founder in 1947 anyway, although it did revamp its prewar Type 57 as a Type 101 and build a few until the early 1950s. Its main interest, however, was as a bearer of coachwork by some of France's great names.

Such coachwork also graced chassis by Delage, Delahaye and Hotchkiss, companies which were all related: Delage had belonged to Delahaye since 1935, and the ailing Hotchkiss was sucked in during 1952. All three makers built traditional chassis styles with engines of between three and four liters, but their market gradually disappeared and, by the mid-1950s, the traditional French *grande routière* was dead.

One manufacturer bravely tried to revive the tradition. Facel Metallon, the builder of special bodies for Panhard, Simca and Ford of France, began building grand touring coupes in 1954 under the Facel Vega name, with enormous American Chrysler engines. Convertibles appeared in 1960, but Facel ran into trouble with the considerably smaller engines it made for these, and even a switch to Volvo and Austin-Healey engines could not save it from going under in 1964.

Preceding pages: The styling of the Citroën DS was almost other-worldly in 1955. This is a 1966 DS21 *décapotable* (convertible), with a 2175cc four-cylinder engine.

Left: This 1952 Bugatti Type 101 represents the last of a dying breed of car – the French *grande routière*. The engine is a twin-cam 3.2-liter six-cylinder; the elegant drophead body is by Gangloff.

Above: The Peugeot four-seater convertibles of the 1950s were well-respected as durable cars. This 403 of 1960 is one of the last of a line introduced in 1956.

Right: The Simca Aronde was a mundane French family sedan until Facel Metallon provided an alternative drophead body style in 1957. The open car was known as the *Plein Ciel*.

Left: Besides building bodies for other manufacturers, Facel Metallon made complete cars under the Facel Vega name. This is a 1961 Facellia, which had the company's own twin-cam 1647cc four-cylinder engine, and a top speed of around 115mph. The striking lines were unfortunately not enough to ensure big sales, as the engine acquired a bad reputation.

Below: Even stodgy sedan-builder Renault tried its hand at open models, dropping the tuned Gordini version of its 845cc four-cylinder engine into this attractive body in 1959 and calling the result a *Floride* (which is French for Florida). Closed coupe versions were also available.

Right: Peugeot's rugged 403 sedans gave way in 1960 to the new 404 models, and open versions appeared at the 1961 Paris Show. Like the sedan, the cabriolet had harmonious styling by the Italian Pininfarina concern. Engines were 1618cc four-cylinders.

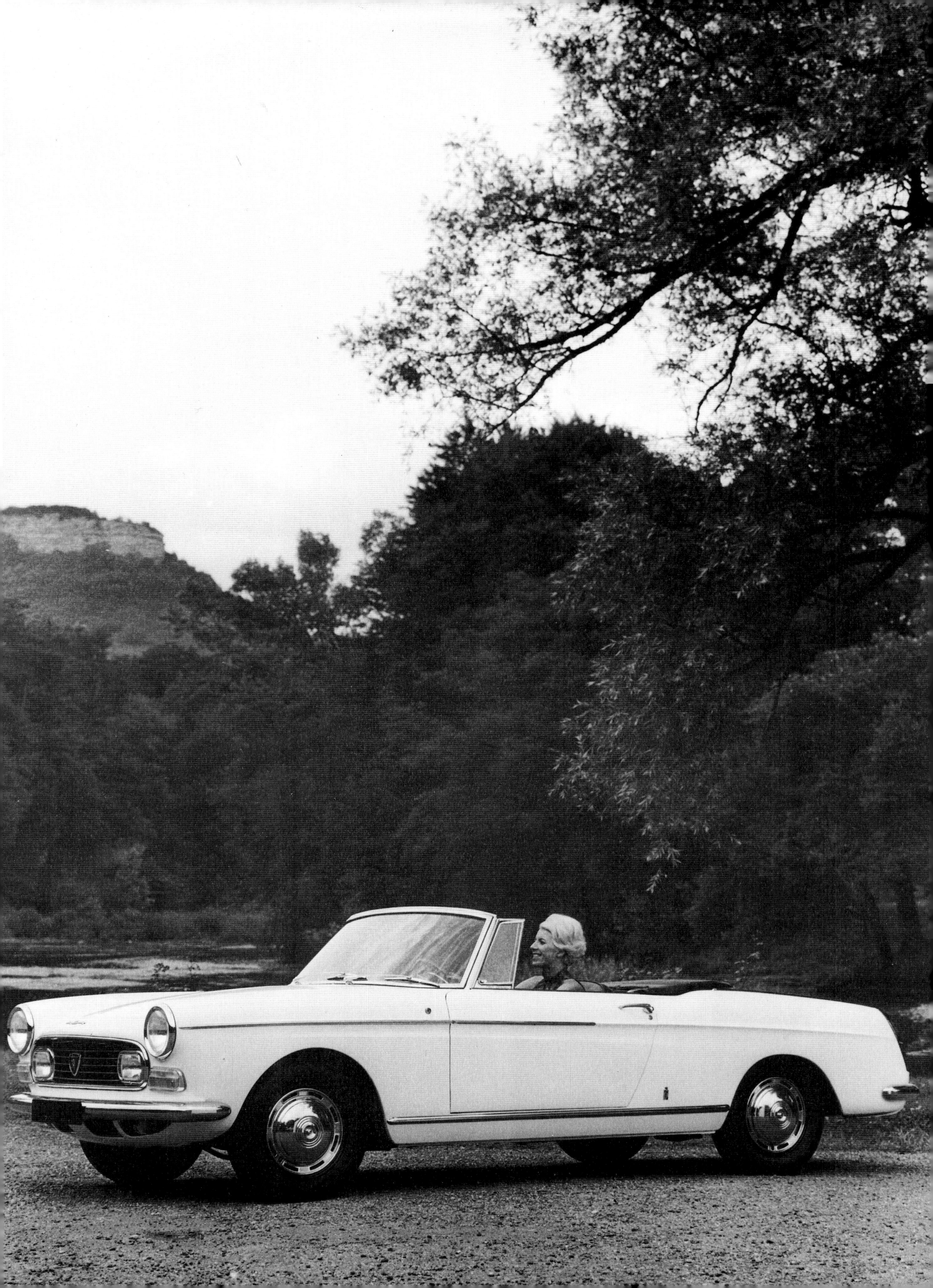

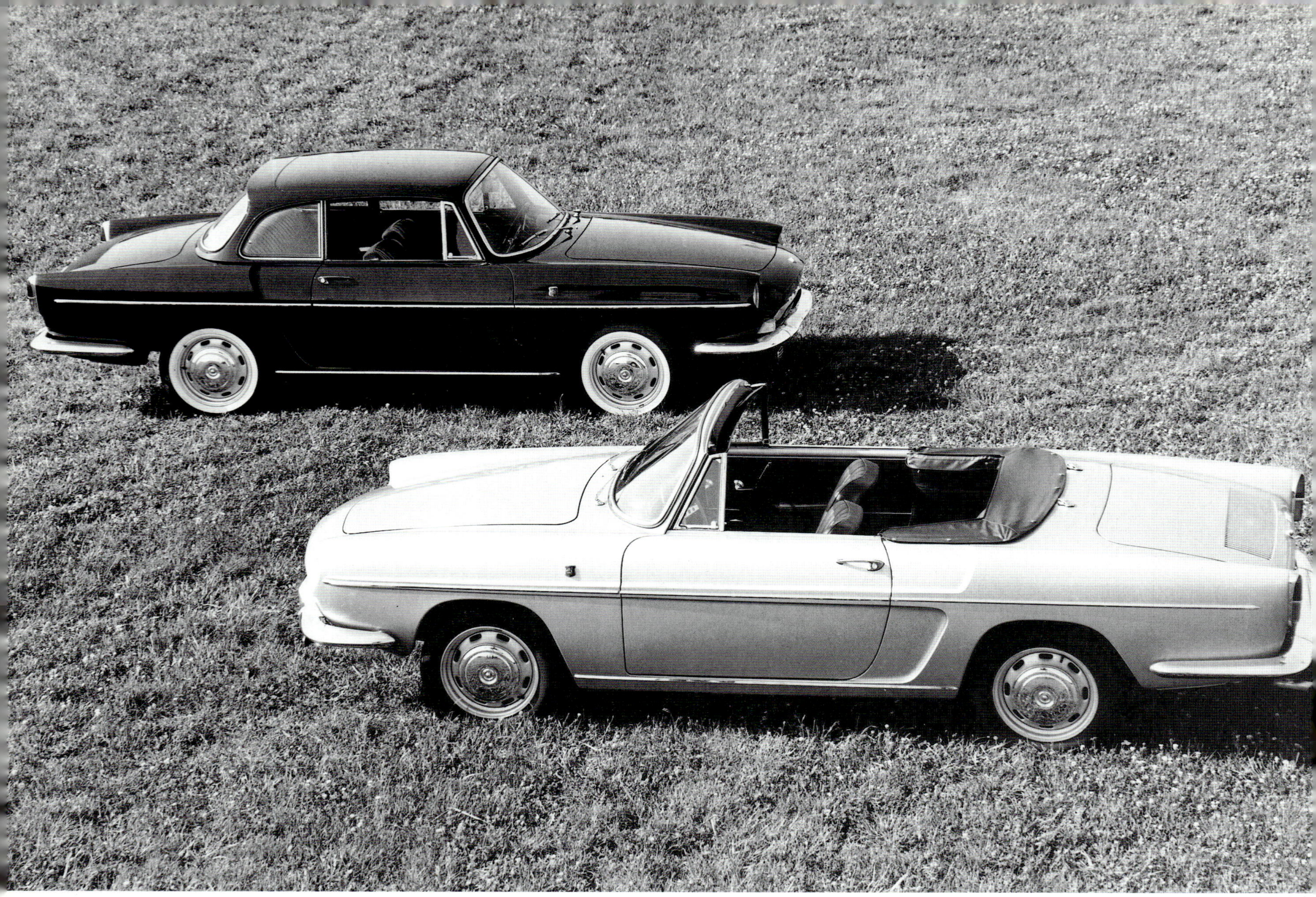

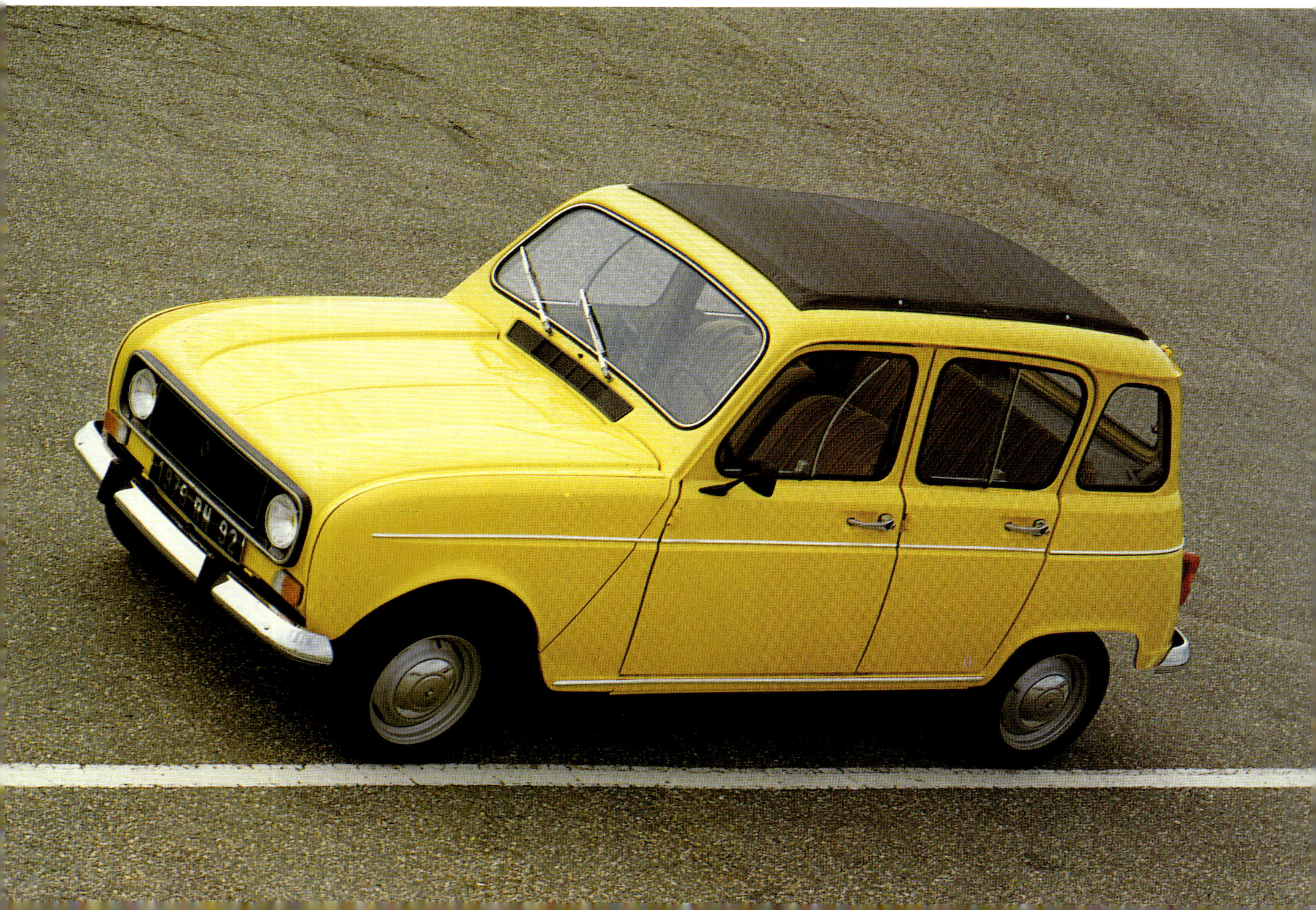

THE FRENCH CONVERTIBLE   57

Top left: Renault replaced the Floride with the Caravelle in 1962. Both performance and seating accommodation were improved, and a closed version was again available alongside the open model. As before, the performance was no match for the car's good looks.

Left: The nearest thing most French car buyers got to a convertible was a sedan with a roll-back roof. Renault again provided this — with the immensely popular little 4 of 1961. Neither sporting nor stylish, it was cheap to run and did offer open-air motoring on demand.

Top right: Peugeot's 204 cabriolet was a pretty two-seater runabout, available from 1966, and based on the 1130cc front-wheel-drive 204 sedan. It was a happy blend of style with modest pretensions.

Right: Peugeot's 404 was replaced by the new 504 in 1968, and from 1969 there was also a beautiful four-seat cabriolet — with styling by Pininfarina, as usual. The first cars had 1796cc engines, but from 1971 a 1971cc type was fitted. Fuel injection was standard throughout, and top speeds were well over 100mph.

58 | CLASSIC CONVERTIBLES

Left: Peugeot's enormously successful 205 hatchback sedan spawned convertible versions in 1986. Note the integral rollover hoop; the main purpose of this was to add rigidity to the body. Several engine types were available. This is a 1.6-liter CTI model, dating from 1990.

Below left: Renault also beheaded one of its small sedans in 1991, and the result was this attractive-looking model. The 1764cc Renault 19 16-valve cabriolet had sparkling performance to match its good looks.

Right: The original Citroën 2CV of 1948 had a roof which rolled all the way back down to rear-bumper level. By the time this 2CV6 Charleston edition was produced in the early 1980s, however, a proper trunk lid and fixed window had reduced the size of the roll-back roof.

Below right: The cabriolet version of the French-built Venturi was announced in 1988. It was a refined sporting car, built in small numbers, and using Renault engines and transmissions. This version has the turbocharged 2.8-liter V6 engine with 260bhp, which was introduced during 1990 and gave a 167mph top speed.

The Sedan-based Convertible

In the early postwar years, several folding-head variants of French sedans appeared, with fixed body side frames but with a full-length opening fabric roof. The type had been popular in the 1930s: Peugeot's revived prewar 202 had such a variant, as did its replacement in 1950, the 203. Renault's little rear-engined 4CV fell into this category too; while the Citroën 2CV came with this style of bodywork only.

Nevertheless, fully-open derivatives of family sedans were available as early as 1946. Peugeot led with the convertible 202 (again a revived prewar model), followed by a convertible 203 in 1951, and then moving up a notch with the 403 in 1956. Facel made some attractive convertible bodies for Simca's Aronde sedans after 1957, but Simca abandoned the convertible market five years later. Renault was content with its folding-head 4CV until 1959, but then announced a new convertible with distinctive styling, based on the sporty Gordini-tuned version of its mundane 845cc Dauphine sedan. This was the Floride, replaced in 1962 by the bigger-engined and slightly restyled Caravelle, which lasted until 1968. Thereafter, however, Renault fought shy of open cars for more than 20 years.

Most of the great French coachbuilders had gone to the wall in the late 1940s and early 1950s, along with the builders of the chassis on whom they had depended for custom. Yet a few lingered on. Chapron experimented in the late 1950s with some low-volume cabriolet conversions of the Citroën DS sedans, and in 1960 the company was chosen to build Citroën's own series-production DS cabriolet. The model remained in production until the early 1970s, but was not replaced. Peugeot, however, turned to the Italian Pininfarina for the styling of all its cars in the mid-1950s, and most of its convertible bodies were also built in Italy. The first Pininfarina convertible for Peugeot was the 403; after that came the sharply-styled 404 of 1961 and the sleek 504 of 1969. Some way farther down the range came the chic little 204 cabriolet, introduced in 1966 and designed by Pininfarina on a shortened 204 sedan floorpan. It was no sportscar, and nor was it intended to be, but as a two-seater it did offer something almost unique on the French market. It was followed in 1972 by the 304S cabriolet, which nevertheless lasted only for four years in production.

The Modern Era

In France, as elsewhere, the 1970s saw a dearth of new convertible designs. Yet there was renewed interest in the 1980s, in the wake of Volkswagen's successful introduction of its Golf cabriolet in 1979. The fastest off the mark was Talbot, with its 1982 Samba convertible based on a small hatchback, although as Talbot was owned by Peugeot, perhaps the credit should be given to France's major mass-producer of convertibles. Once its own 205 hatchback was well established, Peugeot announced a convertible version (again by Pininfarina) in 1986. Citroën, however, stayed clear of the convertible market, while Renault had nothing to offer until 1991's elegant version of the 19 sedan. More ambitious altogether was a new high-performance sportscar called the Venturi, introduced in the mid-1980s as a coupe, but also available in open form from 1988. It was intended mainly for export, however, and was built in small numbers.

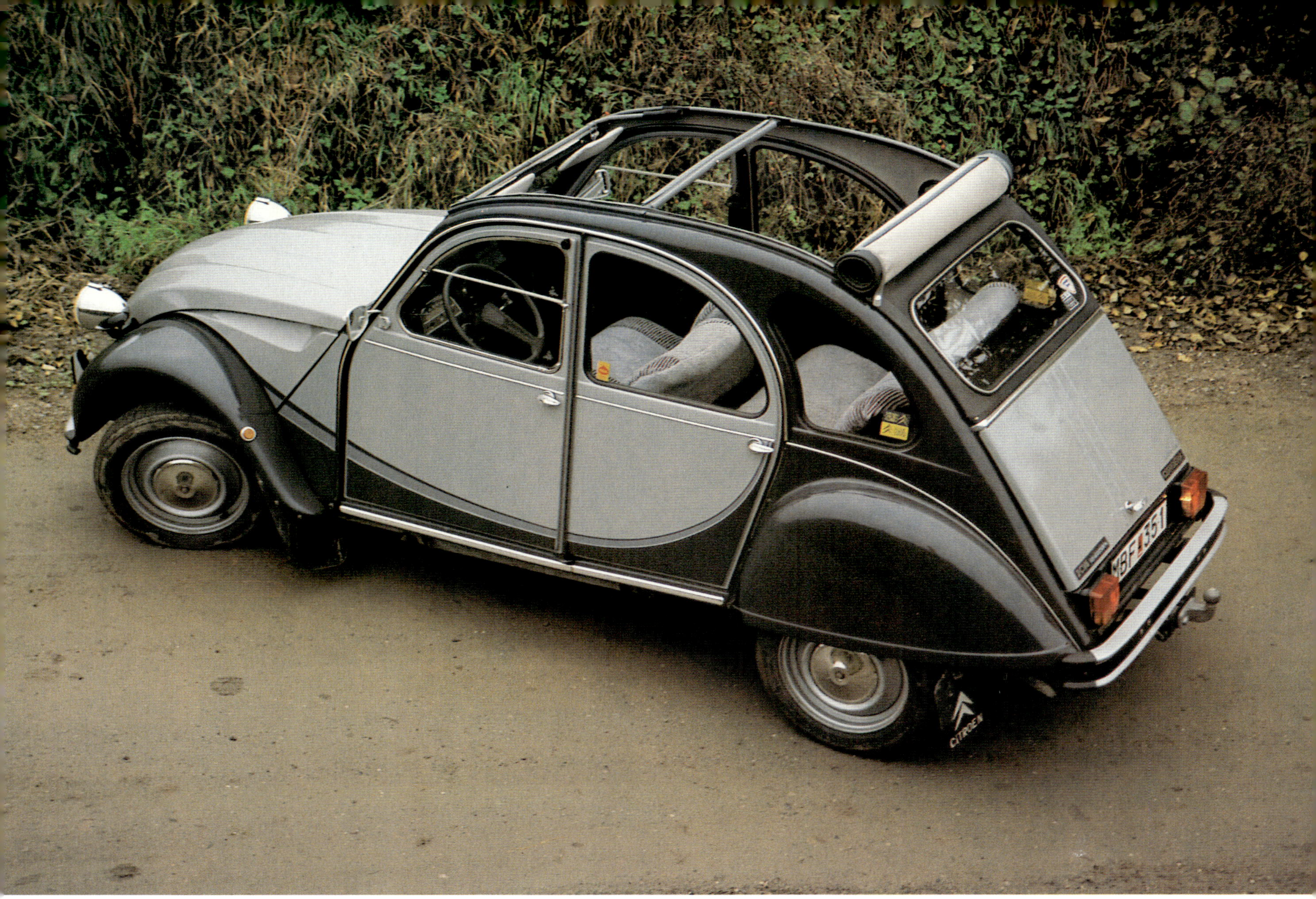

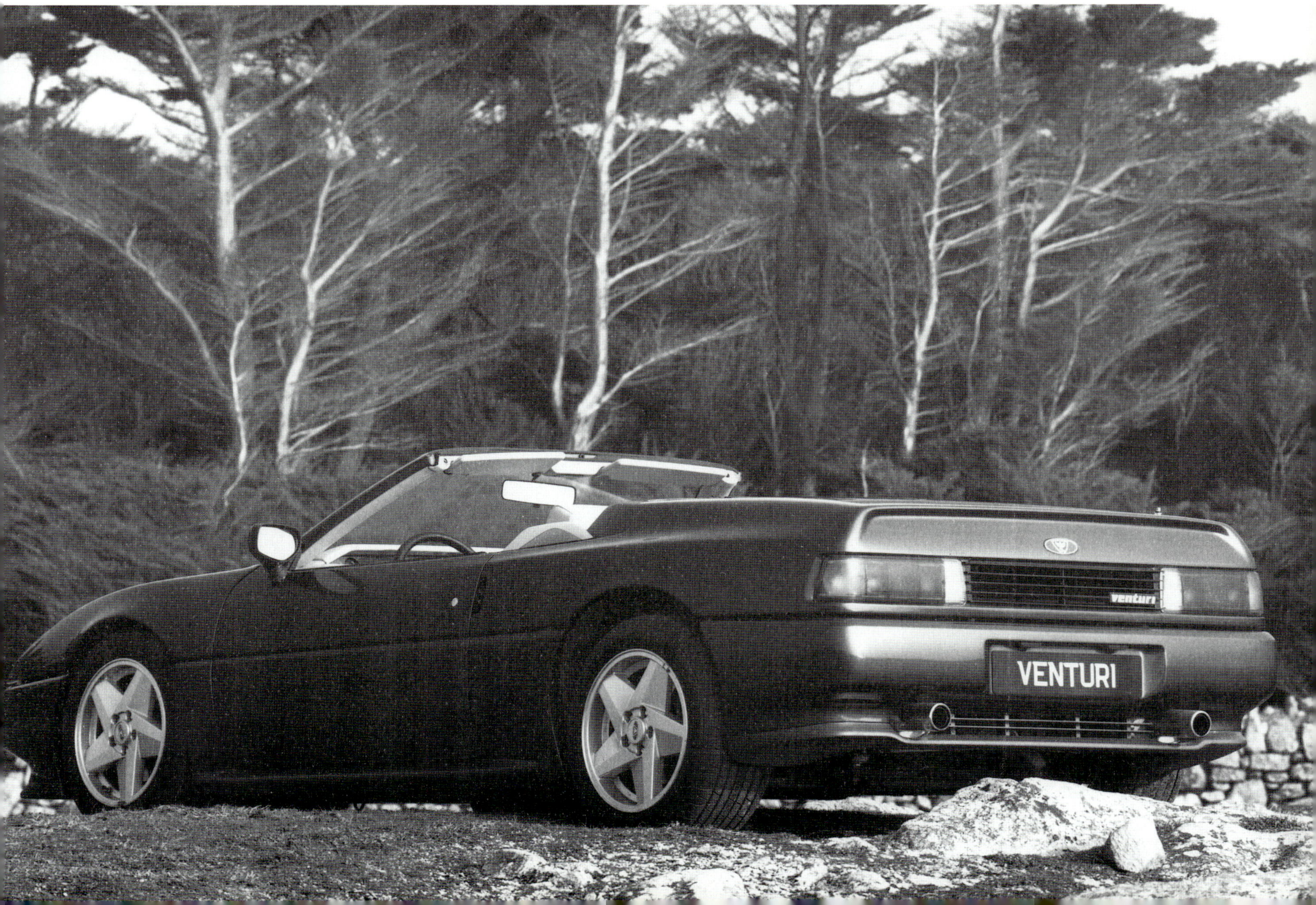
VENTURI

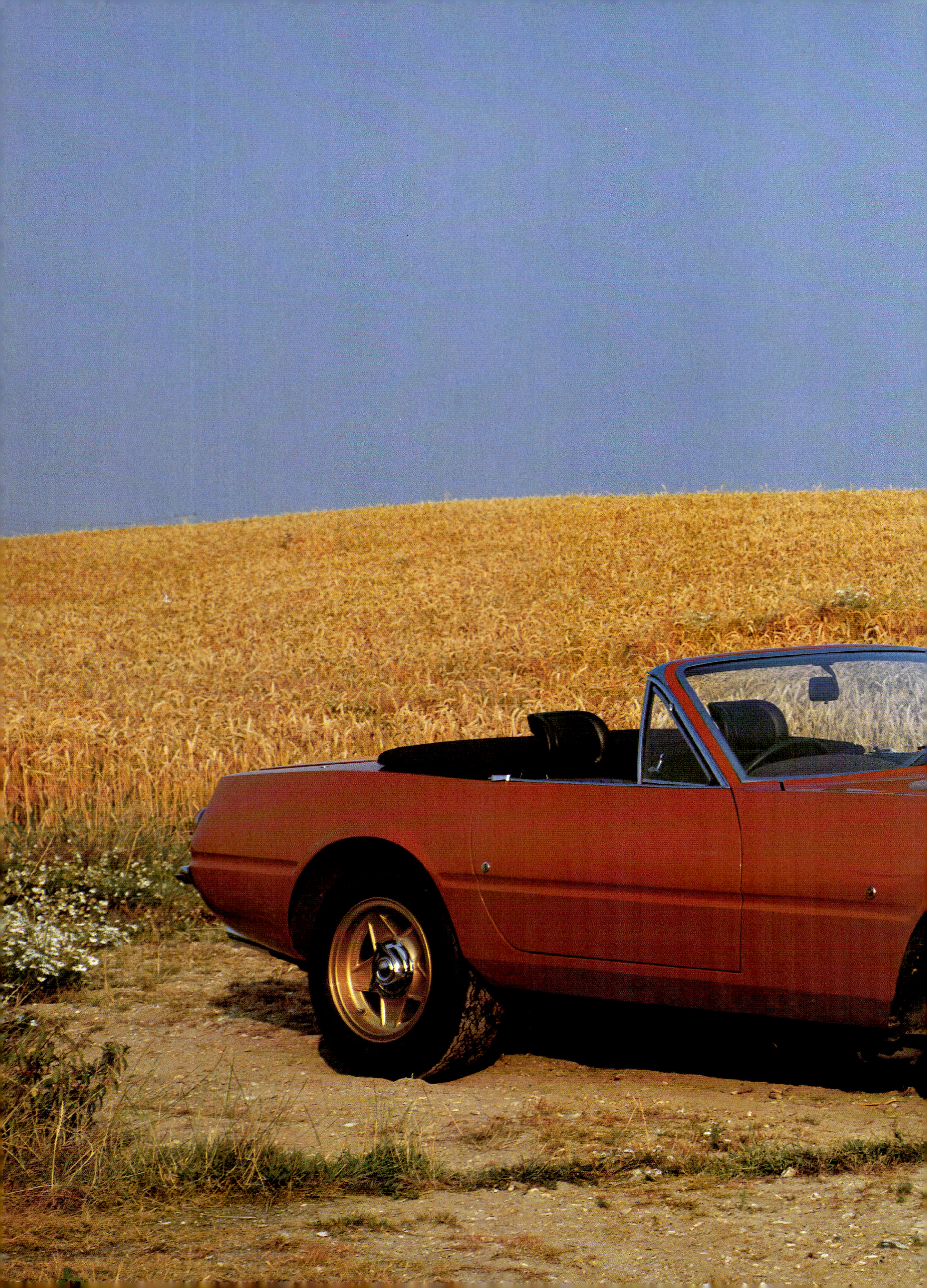

The Italian Convertible

62 CLASSIC CONVERTIBLES

It is tempting to ascribe the large numbers of Italian convertibles built since 1945 to the influence of the Mediterranean climate, but the reality is rather more prosaic. After the war, only three major Italian manufacturers began to build private cars again in the late 1940s: Fiat, Lancia, and Alfa Romeo. The Alfa Romeo was a made-to-order car and was therefore, for most Italians, financially out of the question. The Lancia, too, was an expensive car, beyond the means of all but the wealthier middle classes; and so for most Italians, a Fiat was the only real option. The main model of the late 1940s was the Millecento (1100), which had the advantage of separate-chassis construction. This enabled Fiat customers with a little more than the average endowment of determination and money to go to one of Italy's many coach-building firms and have an individual body built, often for less than the cost of a factory-built Lancia. It was only natural that many of these bodies should be convertibles, traditionally an expression of stylish living.

This trend undoubtedly helped the Italian coachbuilders to survive the gloom of the late 1940s, and it also suggested to the chassis manufacturers that there might be additional profits to be made if they commissioned attractively-styled bodies from the coachbuilders themselves and built these in larger volumes. Thus, by the time unitary construction took over from the separate chassis in the 1950s, it was accepted in Italy that there should be elegant open and closed bodies by the great coachbuilders on offer alongside the standard factory-styled sedans. Although volume-production considerations often prevented the coachbuilders themselves from building the bodies they had designed, their names nevertheless continued to be associated with the more stylish products of the Italian motor industry.

The typical Italian convertible, therefore, has always had more than the usual degree of flair in its styling. On the whole, it has also had a sporting

Preceding pages: One of the most attractive of all open Italian cars was certainly the 1969 Ferrari 365GTS/4, or Daytona spyder. Like all Ferraris, it coupled supercar performance and handling with mouthwatering good looks. The body was styled by Pininfarina.

These pages: Italian coachbuilders are at their best when designing open bodywork. Touring of Milan styled both the 1960 Lancia Flaminia GT 2500 (top left) and the 1958 Alfa Romeo 2000 spyder (bottom left). On the right, both designs are by Pininfarina of Turin. At the top is the 1963 Fiat 1500 cabriolet, while at the bottom is the delightful 1955 Alfa Romeo Giulietta spyder. The two Pininfarina-bodied cars fell into the affordable sportscar category in their native Italy, while the 2-liter Alfa Romeo represented the middle ground, and the Lancia was a wealthy man's car. All of them added sparkling performance to the delights of open-air motoring.

64　CLASSIC CONVERTIBLES

Above: The 1966 Ferrari 365 spyder California was a luxurious cabriolet styled by Pininfarina. The single-cam V12 engine of 4390cc put out 320bhp.

Left: As with all Ferraris, there were several variants of the 250GT spyder California. All had a 2953cc single-cam V12 engine, which developed 250bhp on the car's 1957 introduction and 280bhp by the time the last was built in 1963.

Right: Altogether more affordable than the Ferraris was the Alfa Romeo Giulia GTC cabriolet, with the manufacturer's own bodywork. Styling was workmanlike, but nonetheless successful. The engine was a twin-overhead-camshaft, four-cylinder of 1570cc, which developed 106bhp.

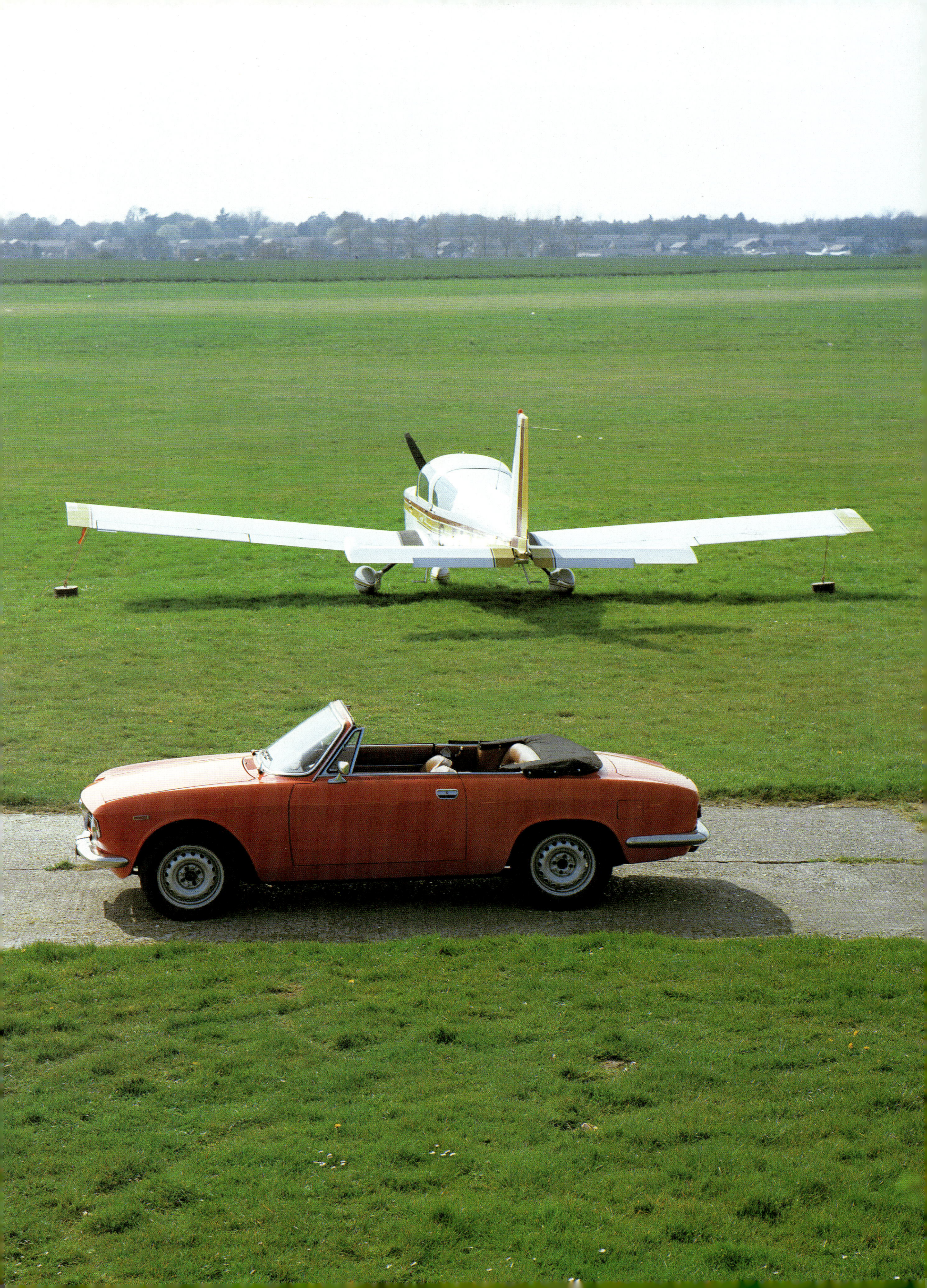

66 CLASSIC CONVERTIBLES

flavor, for the very good reason that Italian manufacturers have attempted to incorporate such characteristics into the basic sedans from which the open cars have been derived. Alfa Romeo employed sporting twin-cam engines to add interest to the mass-produced sedans it was forced to build in order to survive in the early 1950s; Lancia had always had a high-performance orientation; and even Fiat developed twin-cam engines for some of its ranges in the mid-1960s.

Above all these makes, both in price and performance, are the ultra-high-performance convertibles from manufacturers like Ferrari and Maserati. Yet their bodywork has always been styled (and often built) by the same coachbuilders who have worked with lesser makes. It is these cars which have set the standards in their field which other nations' manufacturers have striven to emulate.

Two Liters and Under

In the period after 1945, Italian motor-taxation policies encouraged domestic manufacturers to concentrate on cars with engine capacities of under two liters. In the late 1940s, convertibles in this class began to appear in small numbers: the coachbuilders dressed up humble Fiat Millecento chassis, or collaborated with small companies such as Osca, Abarth and Stanguellini to produce complete cars around tuned Fiat mechanical elements. This process continued throughout the 1950s and 1960s, the mechanical elements often being drawn from the smallest and cheapest Fiats of all – the 500s, 600s, and 850s.

Above: One of Lancia's 2.5-liter V6 engines is under the hood of this Aurelia B24S convertible of the mid-1950s. With 118bhp, the car was capable of 112mph. The svelte styling was by Pininfarina.

Left: The great Italian coachbuilders did not concern themselves exclusively with expensive or exotic cars. Bertone was responsible for the sporty two-seater Fiat 850 spyder, which had no more than 843cc when first announced in 1965. Later examples had a 903cc engine, but none were high-performance cars: 100mph was the absolute limit, and 90mph was kinder to the mechanical elements!

Below left: Lancia's Flaminia was very much an upper-crust model in Italy. The first open models in 1959 had 2.5-liter V6 engines, but from 1963 a larger 2755cc V6 was standard. These Touring-bodied cars were good for 112mph in original form, and for 120mph by the time production ended in 1967.

Top right: Two extremes of the Fiat range are represented here. At the top is the Dino, introduced in 1967 and powered by a Ferrari-designed 1987cc V6 with twin overhead camshafts. Despite a top speed of 160mph and its exotic appearance, it was not a strong seller. Altogether less pretentious was the 124 spyder (right), introduced in 1966 and featuring attractive but understated Pininfarina styling and twin overhead camshafts on its 1438cc four-cylinder engine. By the time of the 1969 example pictured, the engine capacity had gone up to 1608cc and performance had been improved.

By the mid-1950s, however, the major manufacturers had recognized the value of having what would today be called 'designer' bodies in their ranges, and sports convertibles styled by the major coachbuilders began to appear in series-production form. Typical were the 1954 Alfa Romeo 1900 Super Sport and the 1955 Alfa Romeo Giulietta spyder, both styled by Pininfarina; Lancia's 1957 Appia cabriolet by Vignale also fell into this category. Pininfarina was responsible for the body of the 1959 Fiat Osca 1500S (which had an Osca twin-cam engine allied to its Fiat floorpan and running gear), and the same body continued on different Fiats until 1967. Pininfarina was again called upon for 1966's Fiat 124 spyder, but it was Bertone who styled the little Fiat 850 spyder of 1965, Bertone who came up with the wedge-shaped styling for the mid-engined, Targa-top Fiat X1/9 in 1973, and Bertone who turned the unattractive Ritmo hatchback (known as a Strada in some markets) into a convertible for Fiat in 1979.

Touring was responsible for the 1958 Alfa Romeo 2000 spyder, but it was Pininfarina who drew up one of the longest-lasting sporting-convertible styles. Introduced in 1966, his Alfa Romeo Duetto is still in production today, albeit with updated power-train elements and revised styling. It was Pininfarina, too, who styled the Targa-top bodywork for Lancia's 1974 Beta spyder, available until 1982 with a range of engines from 1600cc to 2000cc. Nevertheless, the major Italian manufacturers have introduced no new convertibles for the 1980s or 1990s in the sub-two-liter category, and are no doubt still waiting for signs from America that the market for such cars is recovering before they do so.

Lastly in this smallest category, there have been Fiat's folding-top economy sedans – the 500 in its original and revised (1957) form, and its larger 600 stablemate. This type of convertible died out in 1970, however.

Convertibles for the Wealthy

As the taxation on cars with engines larger than two liters was heavy, those convertibles which fell into this class were aimed at wealthy customers. It therefore followed that such cars were also generally better equipped than their smaller brethren. They were, of course, quite different from the ultra-high-performance supercars built by certain Italian manufacturers.

Predominant in this market, while it lasted, was Lancia. The company's first postwar convertibles had arrived in 1955, in the shape of the delicious Aurelia B24 models, with Pininfarina styling and 2.5-liter V6 engines. Relatively few were made in three years of production, and the Flaminia GT convertibles by Touring which followed maintained the tradition of exclusivity.

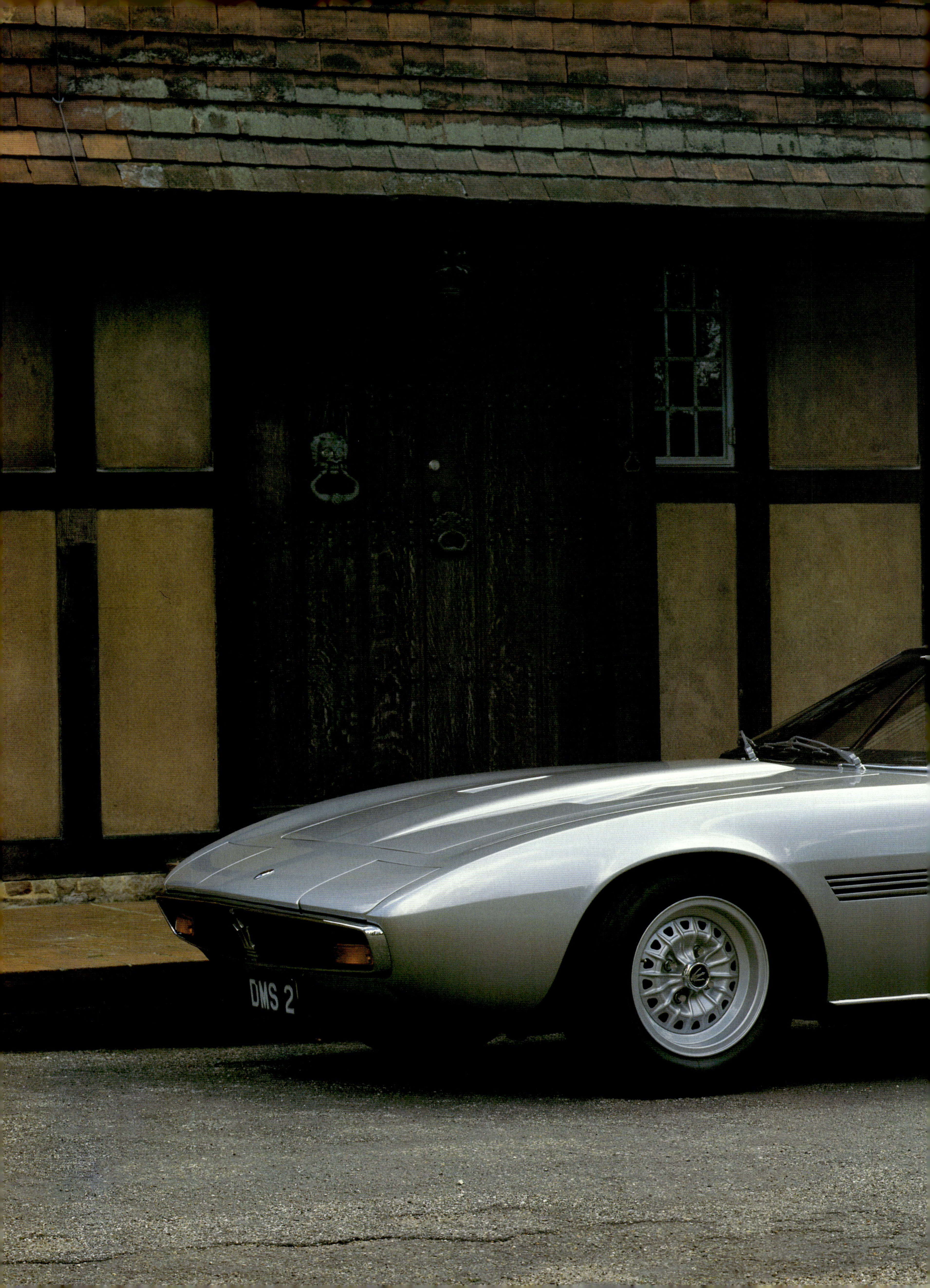
DMS 2

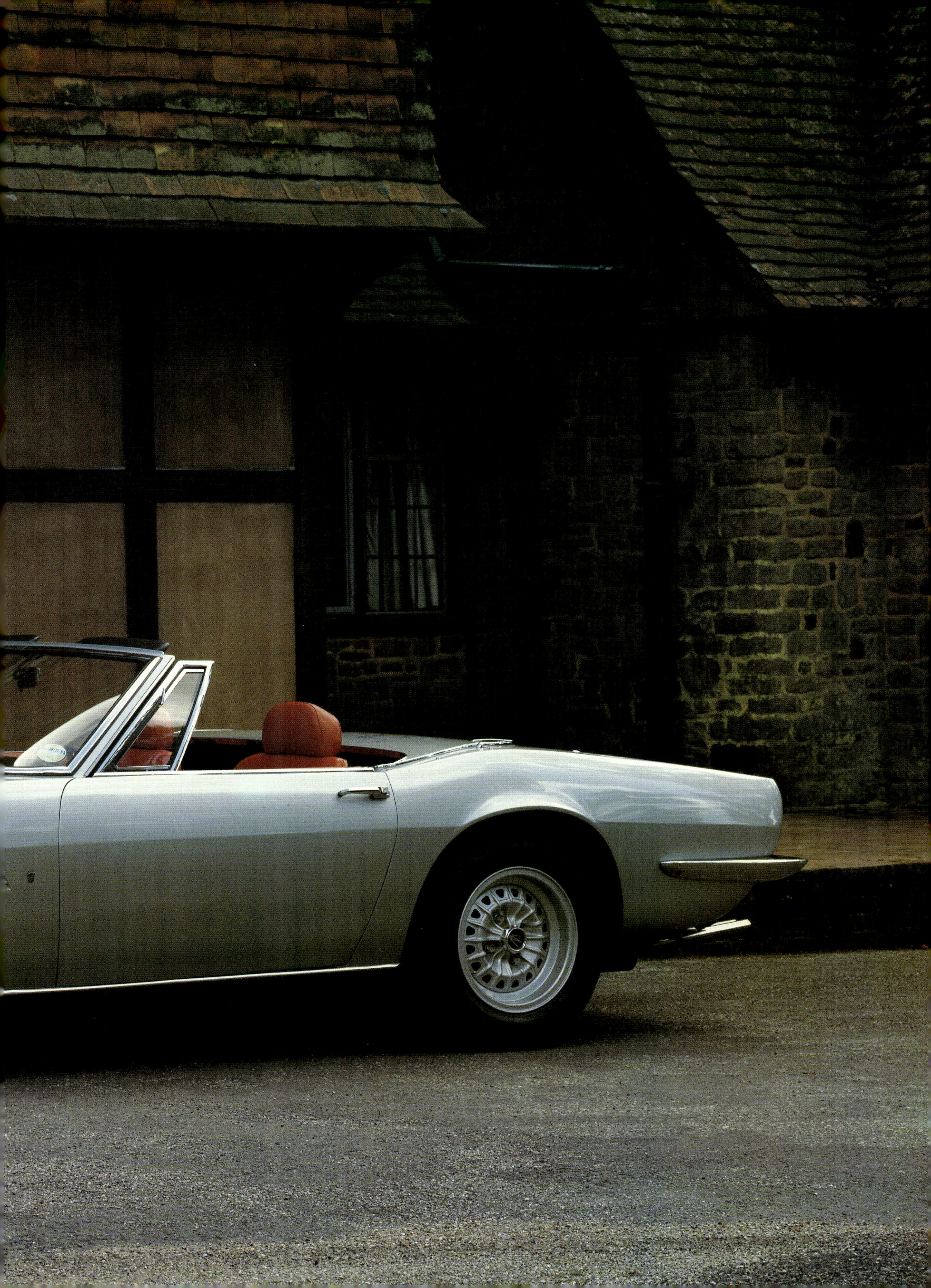

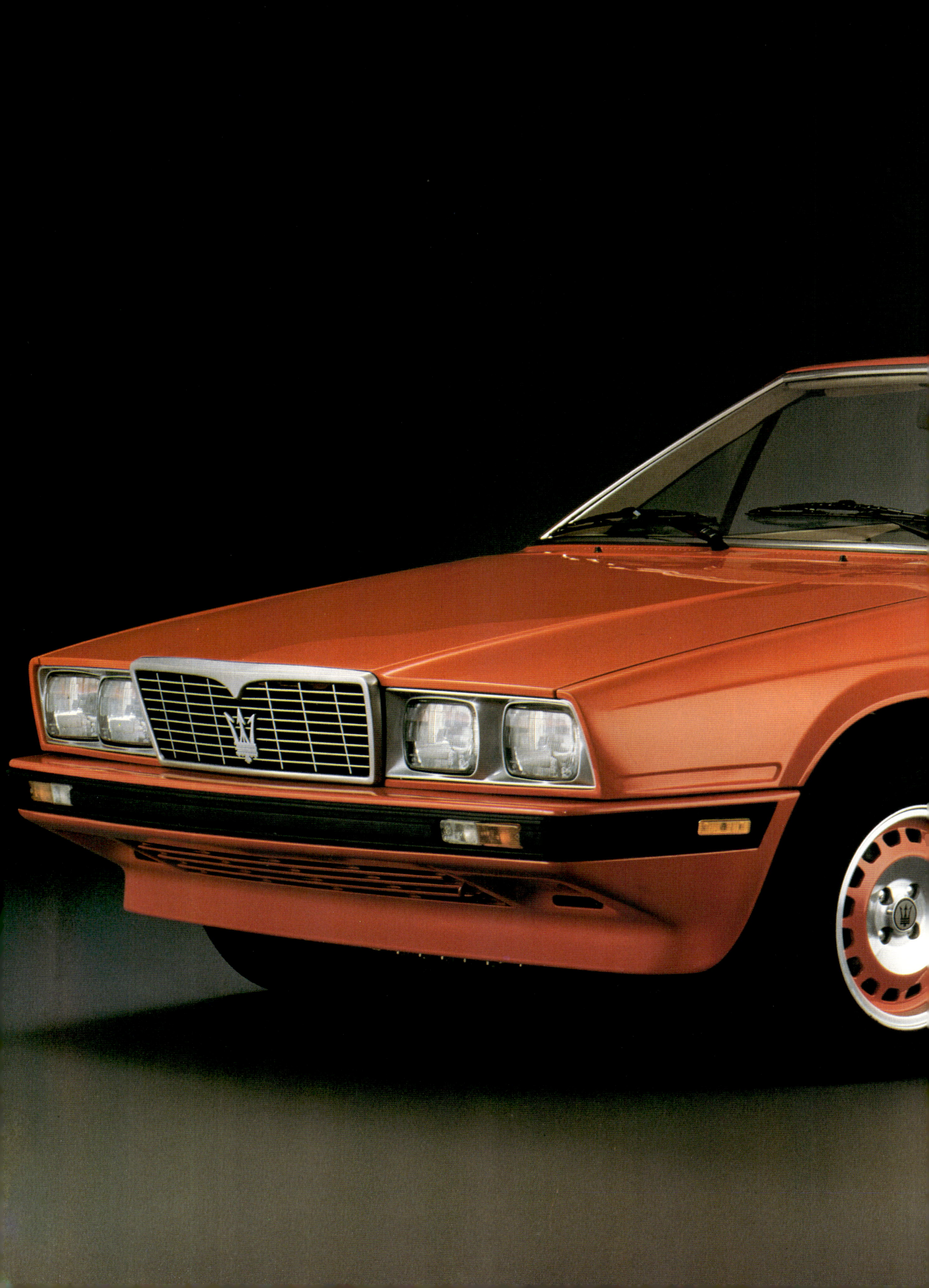

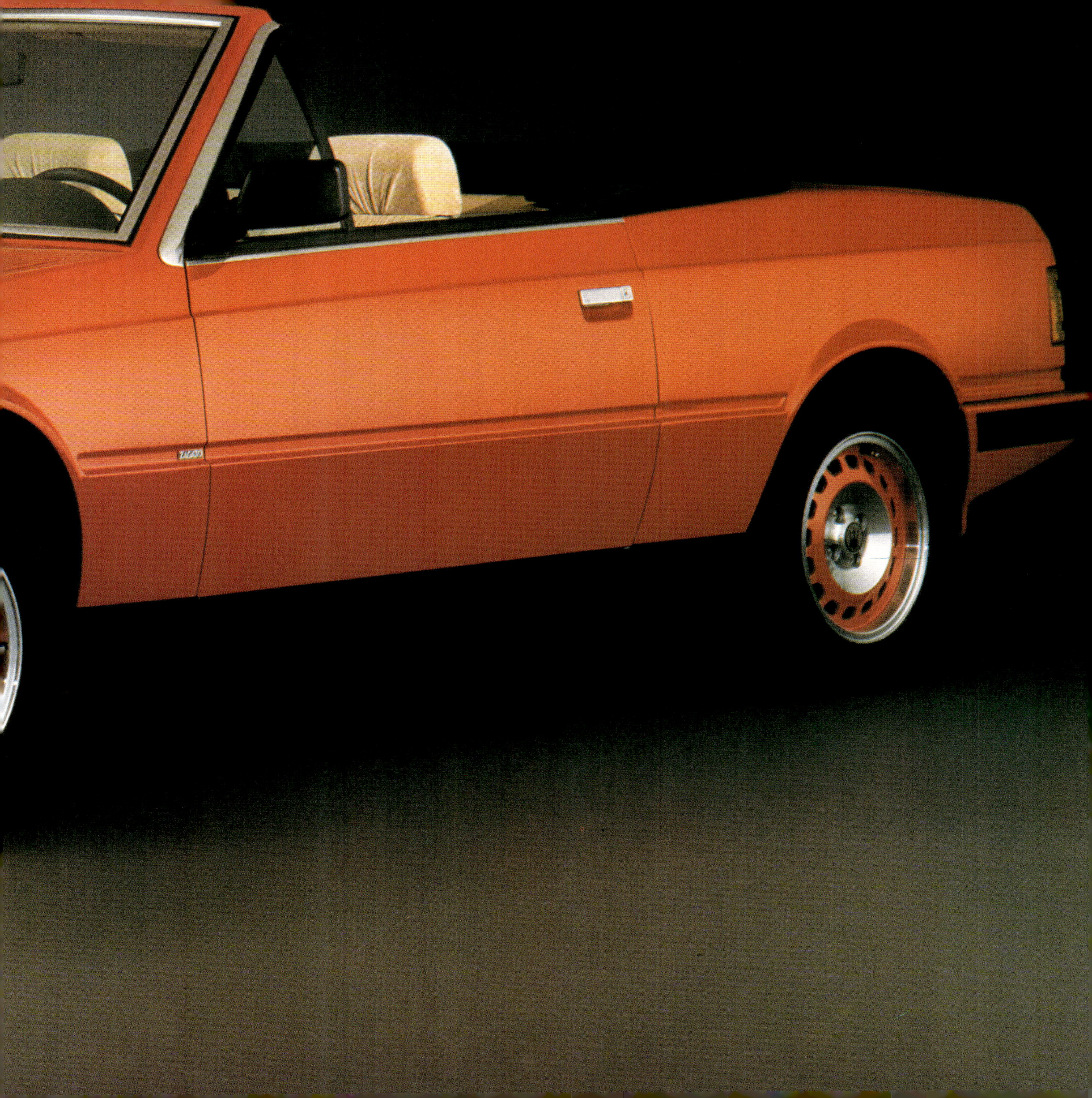

Pages 68-69: The Maserati Ghibli was a supercar of its time, with a top speed of more than 170mph. Introduced in 1967, it could be had in either open or closed form, in both cases with styling by Ghia. The V8 engine had four overhead camshafts and a capacity of 4719cc, which was later increased to 4930cc.

Pages 70-71: The convertible version of Maserati's Biturbo coupe appeared in 1984. Its styling was remarkably restrained for a manufacturer noted for its exotic supercars, and the engine was a radical departure from the big V12s and V8s associated with Italian exotica: it was a 2-liter with twin turbochargers. Nevertheless, it sold well and brought Maserati a profit, allegedly for the first time in the company's history!

Left: The Ferrari 400i was introduced in 1979 and remained in production until 1985. Styling was by Pininfarina and the car normally came as a two-door, four-seater coupe. In the search for something different, however, the owner of this example had his car turned into a drophead. All the 400i models had fuel-injected twin-cam V12 engines of 4823cc.

Right: Since the demise of the Daytona spyder in 1973, open Ferraris had employed Targa tops. With the launch of the Mondial cabriolet in 1984, however, the marque again boasted a real convertible. Once more the styling was by Pininfarina; the engine was a quad-cam V8 of 2927cc and 230-240bhp.

Alfa Romeo tried to break into this market sector in 1962 by dropping a 2.6-liter six-cylinder engine into its existing four-cylinder Touring-bodied 2000 spyder, but the move was not a profitable one. Exclusivity did not pay the bills, and after 1963 the Italian manufacturers deserted the middle ground for convertibles, clustering instead in the sub-two-liter market or moving upward into the supercar class.

The Supercars

The great Italian supercar tradition really began with Alfa Romeo, whose 6C-2500, announced just before World War II, was reintroduced to the market when peace returned. Yet Italy's economic conditions could not support such expensive cars, all of which had coachbuilt bodies, and from 1950 Alfa Romeo was obliged to turn to the mass production of family sedans and cheaper sporting models in order to survive. Later supercar contenders from Alfa Romeo – the 1970 Montreal and the 1990 SZ – came in closed form only, and their performance was below that of the established supercars of their times.

The initiative passed from Alfa Romeo in the late 1940s to one of the company's former employees. Enzo Ferrari had set up in business in 1940, and in 1948 he began producing high-performance cars based on superb V12 engines. The earliest Ferraris were largely handbuilt to order, with performance levels way above those of almost any other car on the road – and prices to match. The bodywork was always by one or other of the leading Italian coachbuilders, and many exquisite convertibles were constructed in the 1950s and 1960s. Gradually, however, 'standard' production models took the place of the made-to-order cars of earlier times, and the 1970s saw Targa-top models replace full convertibles. When convertibles did return in 1984, they remained much less common than before, and Ferrari's customers showed the same preference for the closed models which was evident at all levels of the market worldwide.

Ferrari's main domestic competitor was Maserati, which had been primarily a racing-car manufacturer before 1957. After that date it turned to high-performance roadgoing models, most of which were bodied as coupes by the great Italian coachbuilders, although several convertibles were built. Open cars disappeared during the 1970s, but when they returned with the Biturbo in 1984, the Maserati was no longer in the same supercar league as Ferrari's products.

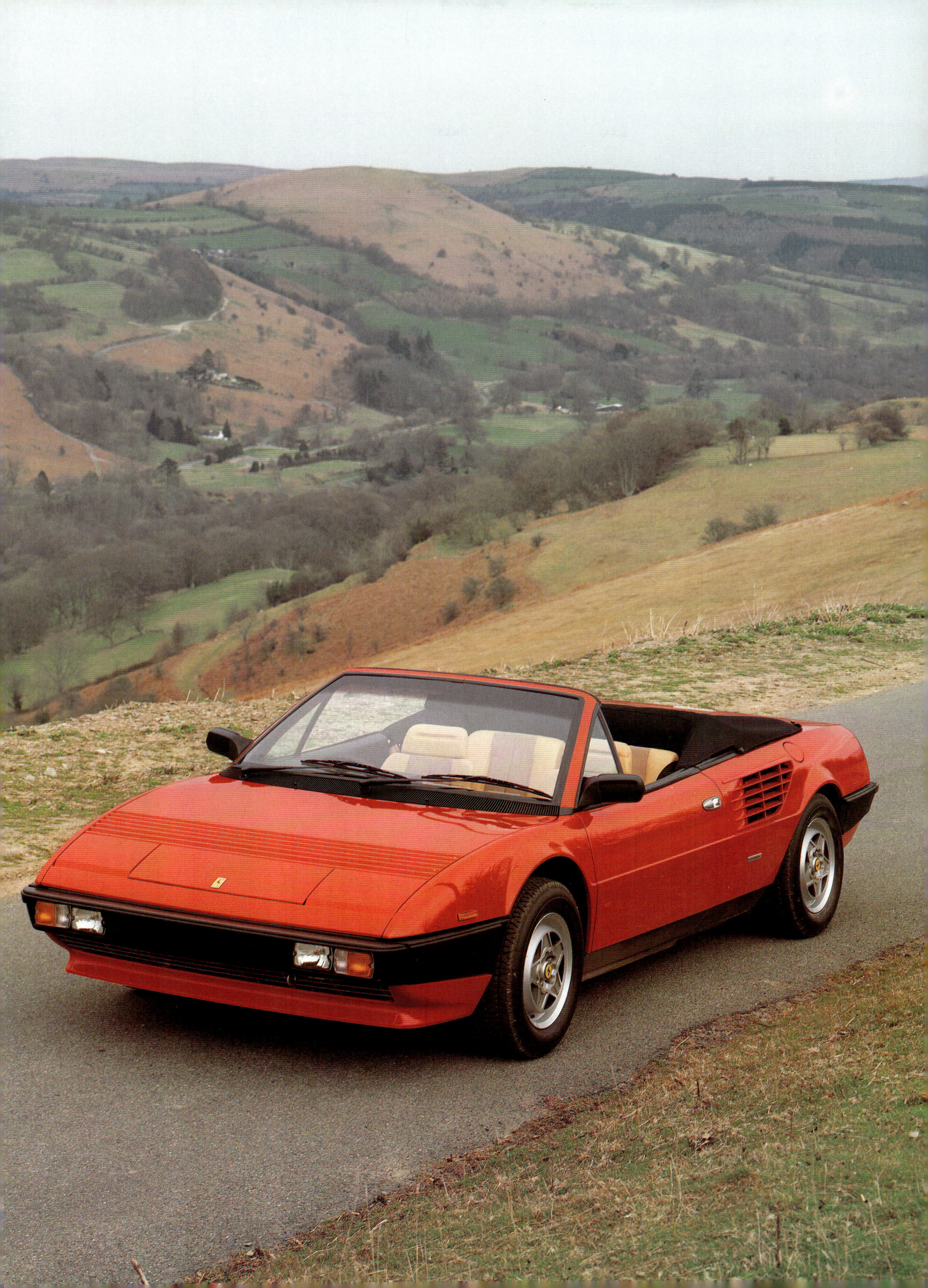

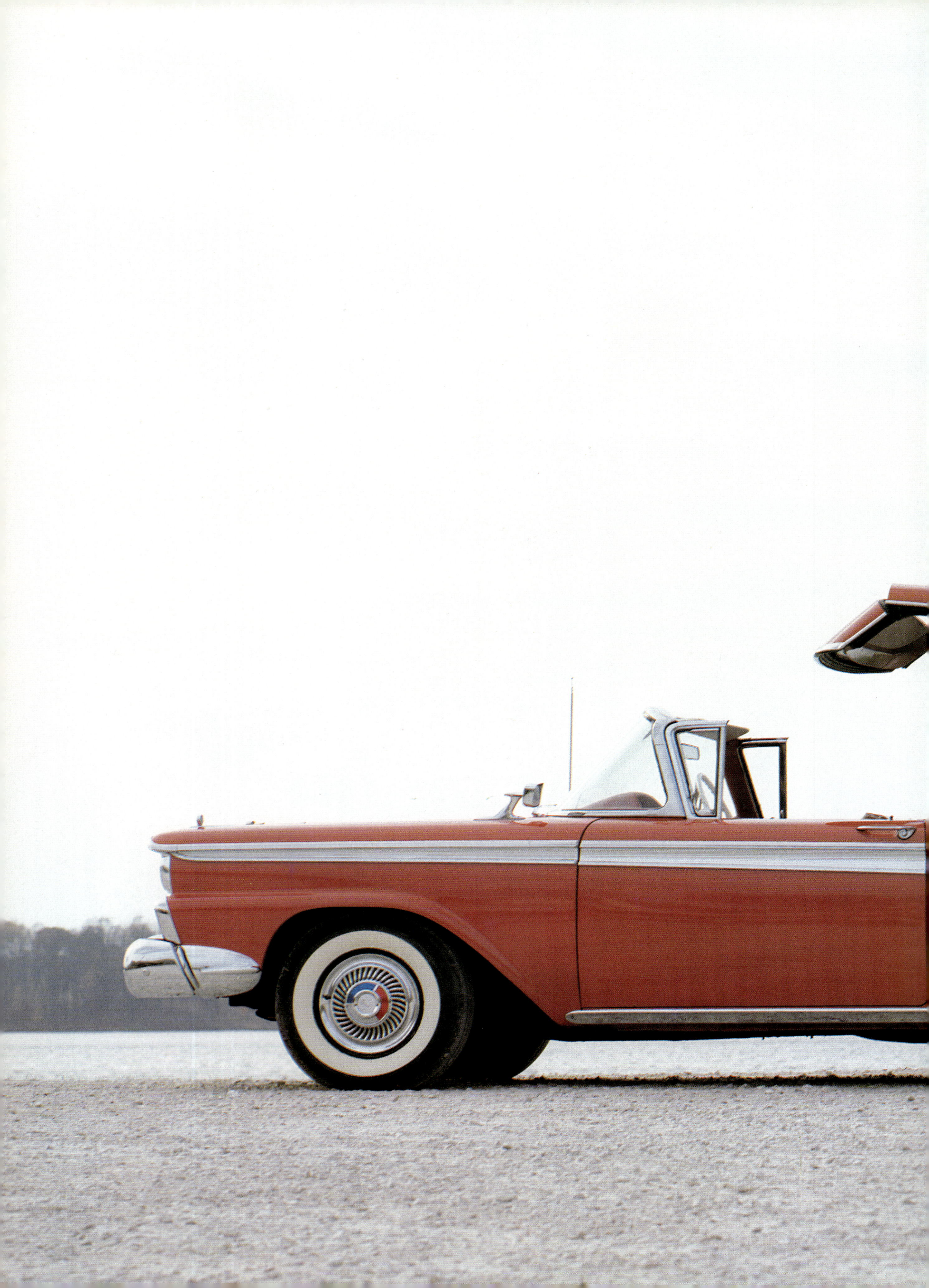

The American Convertible

76 CLASSIC CONVERTIBLES

When World War II ended, the American economy was not in the same parlous state as those of the European protagonists, and so the country did not have to suffer the same period of austerity at the end of the 1940s. Convertible versions of the standard-sized American car had been popular in the 1930s, and the buying public expected them to return alongside ordinary sedans as soon as car production resumed. For all these reasons, the American motor manufacturers had convertibles in production as early as 1945, although the cars were, in fact, revived 1942 models rather than new designs.

American convertibles were always big cars by European standards, just as the sedans on which they were based dwarfed the average European sedan. Cars like these were built continuously from 1945 until the mid-1970s, without being unduly affected by the rising tide of European imports during the 1950s. However, the success of European open sportscar two-seaters in the United States did provoke General Motors into creating a new type of car in the shape of the 1953 Chevrolet Corvette. Although it tackled the European two-seaters directly in appeal and on price, it was in many ways a very different kind of car, altogether more finely judged to suit the longstanding preferences of American buyers.

The Corvette set off a chain reaction. In the longer term, instead of undermining the European imports, it created its own highly lucrative market, and this provoked other American manufacturers into developing new models. Within two years Ford had decided to cream off some of the Corvette's buyers, and its 1955 Thunderbird open two-seater, although perhaps less

Preceding pages: One of the cars most evocative of the American convertible's golden age was not a convertible in the usual sense of the term. The Ford Galaxie Skyliner retractable hard top was exactly that – and in this picture the power-operated top is seen on its journey into the trunk. The car is a 1959 example.

These pages: American manufacturers were quick off the mark with new convertibles after the end of World War II. The top picture here shows a 1947 Buick convertible, with the 110bhp straight-eight engine. Even the cheaper Buick convertibles had power-operated tops, windows and front-seat adjusters, although performance was not a strong point. The lower picture shows Ford's attempt to capture a slice of the luxury-car market, then dominated by Packard and Cadillac. The 1948 Lincoln Continental cabriolet had a 125bhp V12 engine of 292 cubic inches, but sold disappointingly.

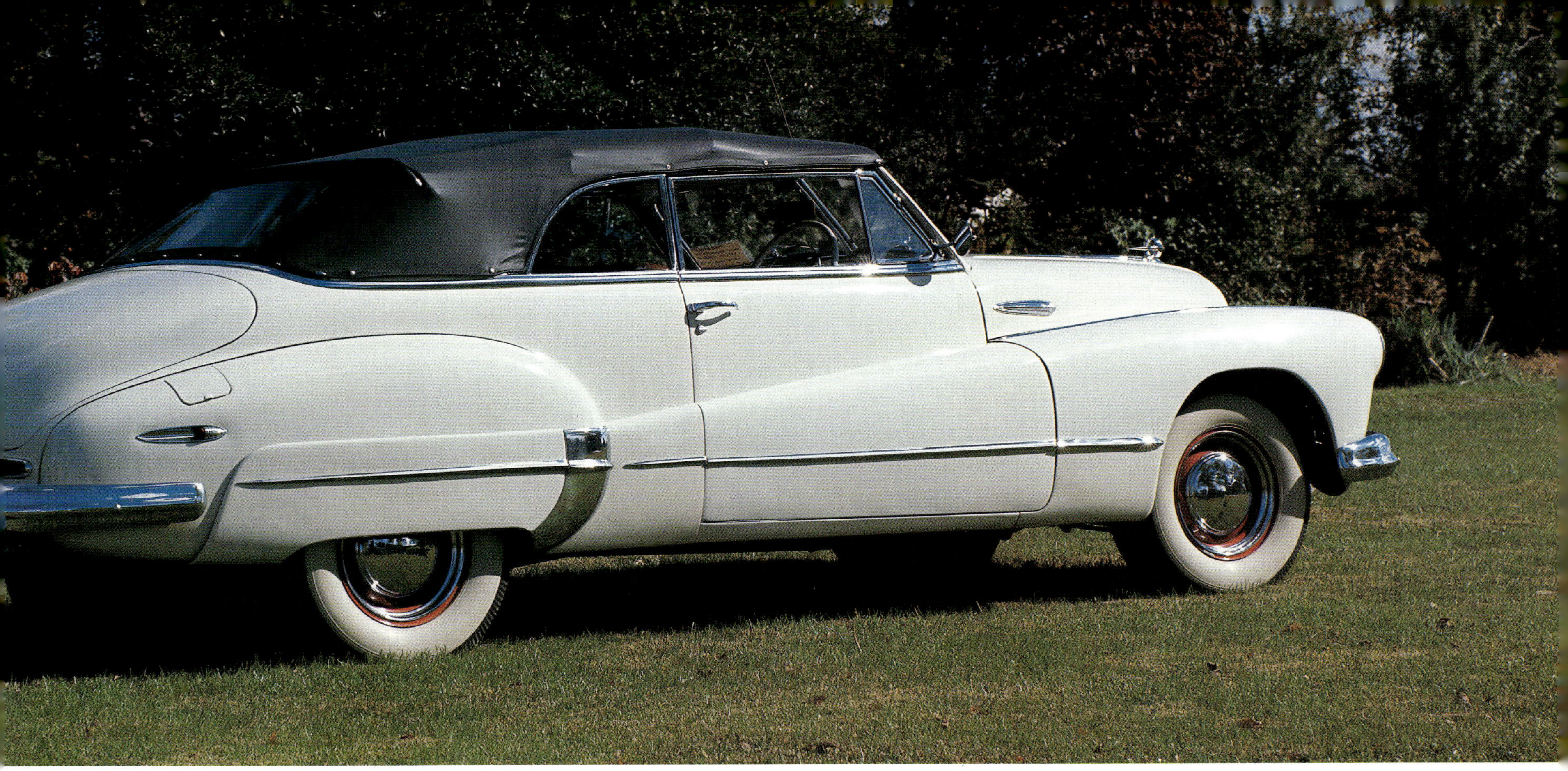

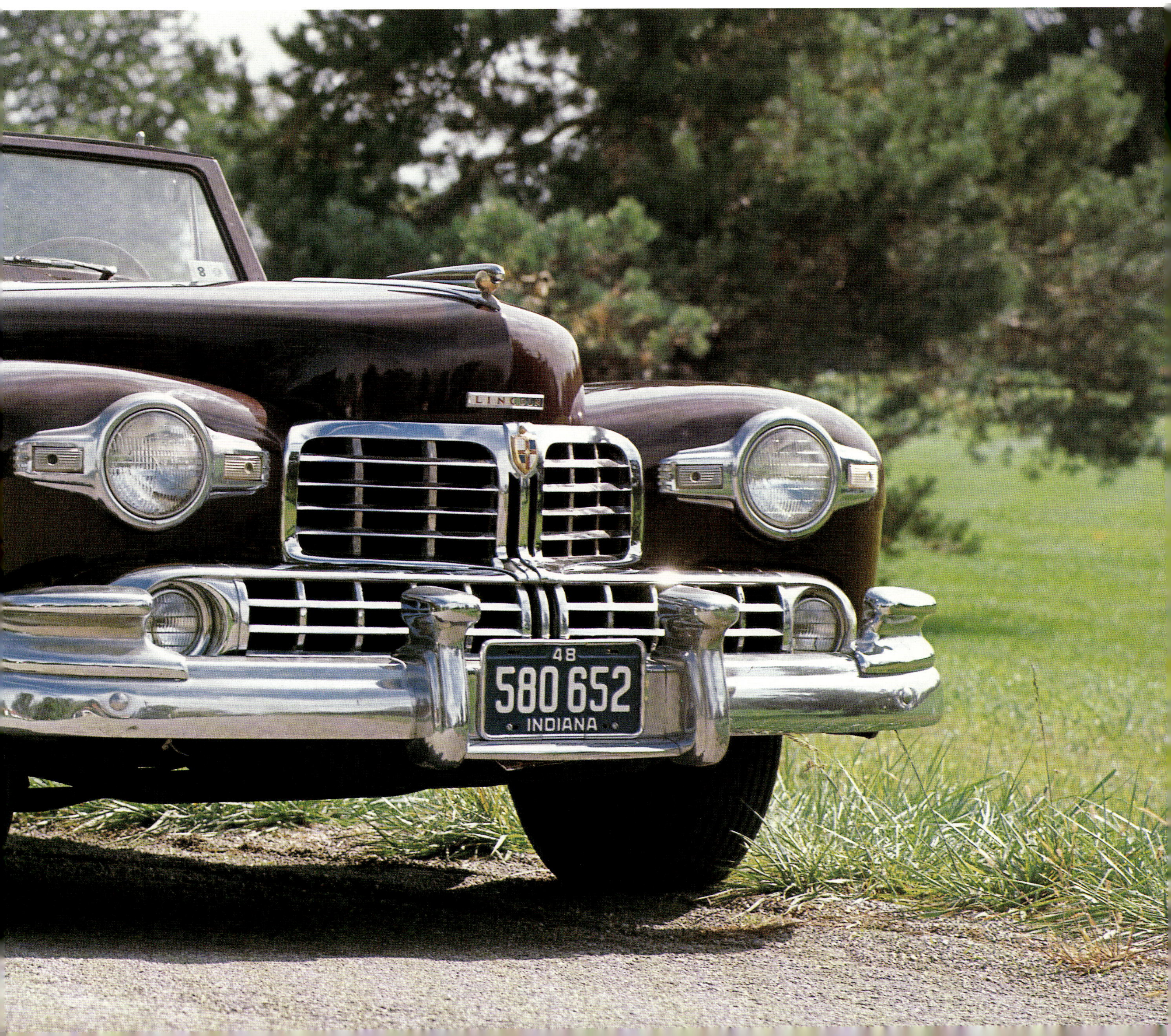
48
580 652
INDIANA

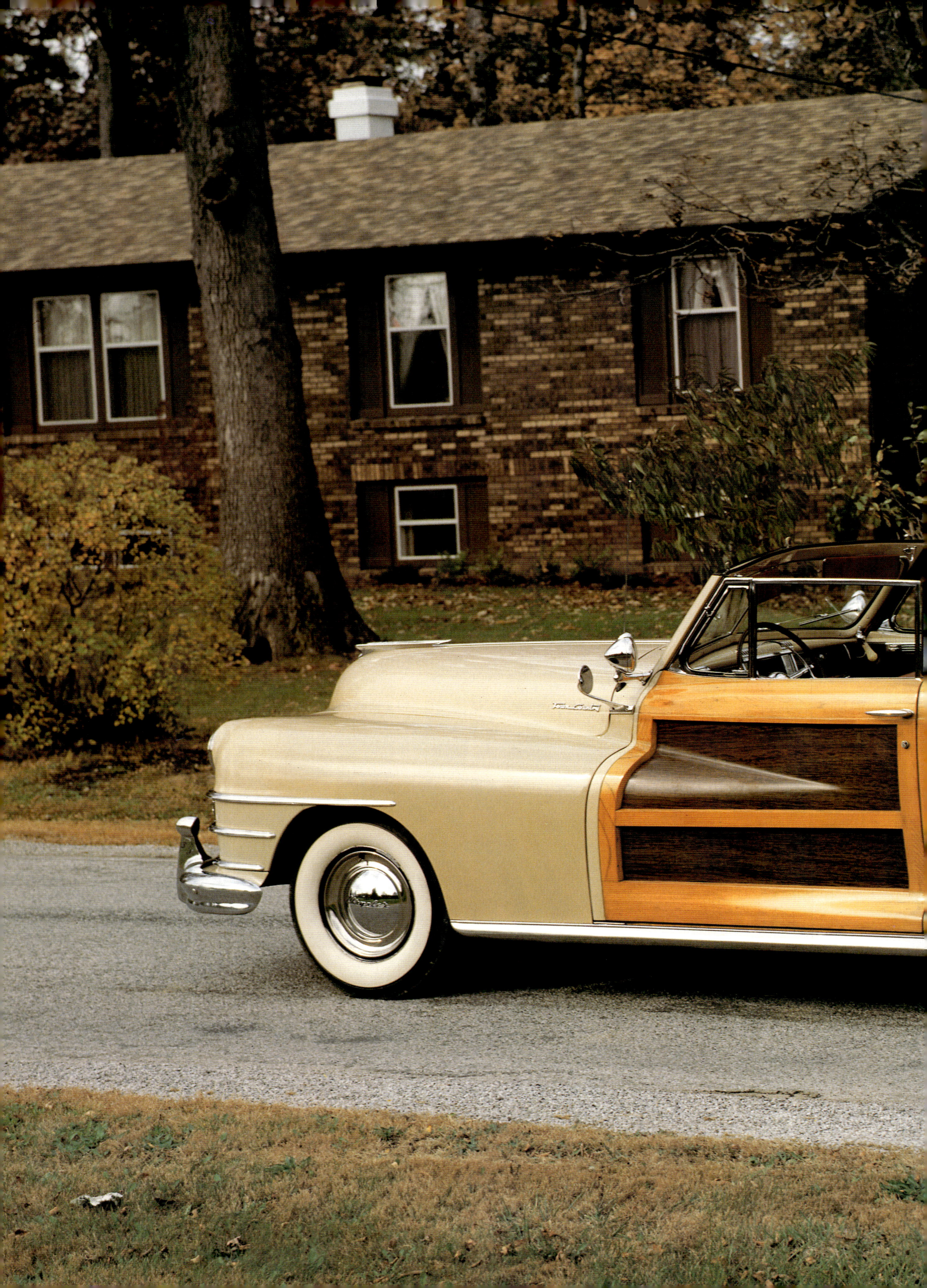

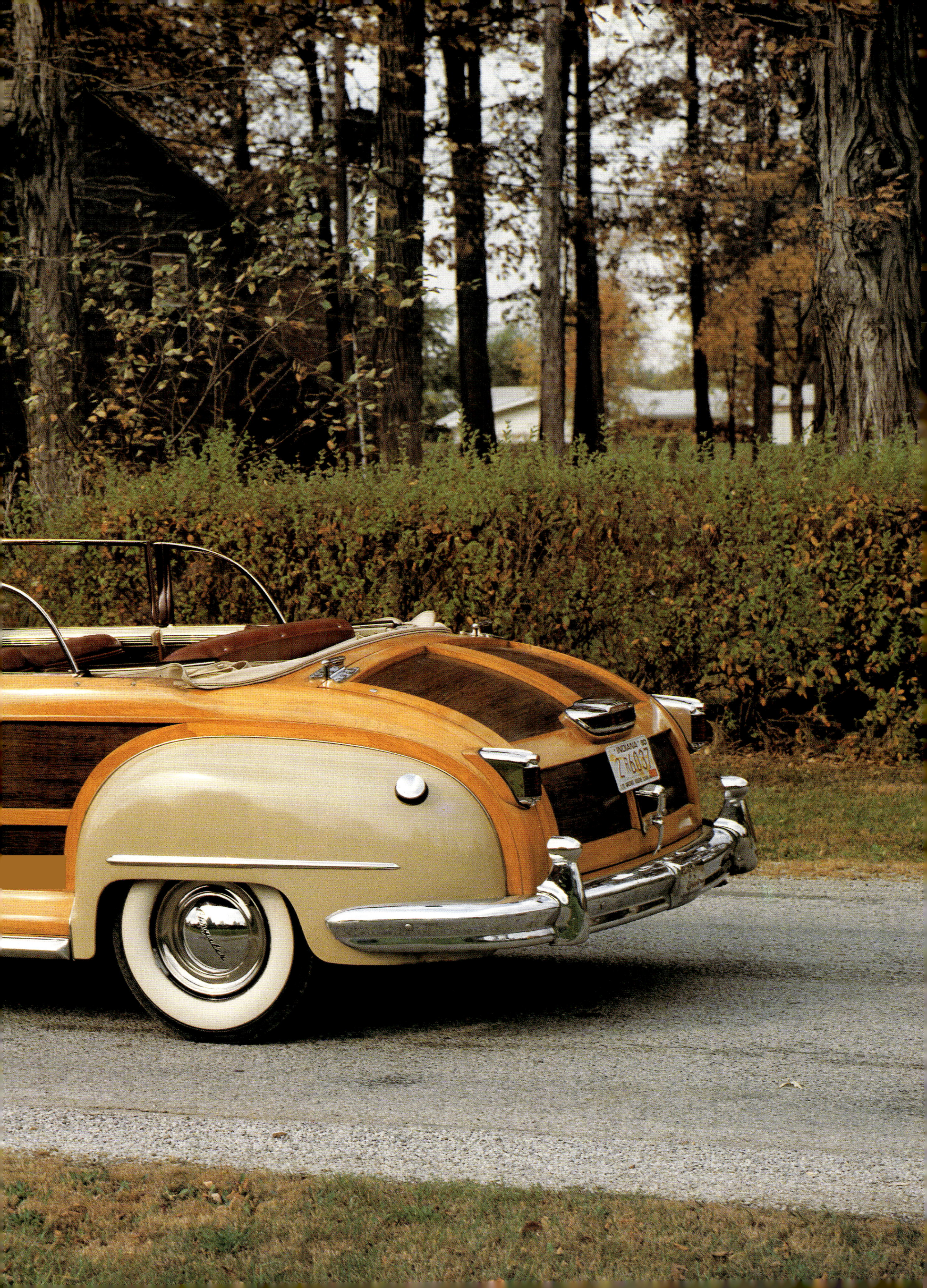
INDIANA
ZR6037

80 CLASSIC CONVERTIBLES

THE American Convertible 81

Preceding pages: Chrysler's Town and Country convertibles were nothing if not distinctive. By the time of this 1948 example, fake wood trim had replaced the real wood seen on earlier cars, in an attempt to keep costs down. The 323.5 cubic-inch straight-eight engine gave 135bhp.

Left: The Chevrolet Corvette was strictly a roadster for its first few years, but wind-up door-windows appeared in 1956 and were a feature of all subsequent models. This is a 1959 car, with a 283 cubic-inch (4.6-liter) V8 engine.

Above: The 1948 Packard Custom Eight Victoria convertible coupe was a hugely expensive luxury model with a 160bhp straight-eight of 356 cubic inches. The 1948 Packards received a styling award from New York's Fashion Academy.

Right: By the time this car was built in 1953, Cadillac had taken over from Packard as America's premier luxury-car builder. The Eldorado convertible introduced new rakish styling, and had a massively powerful 210bhp V8 engine of 331 cubic inches. Just 532 examples of this limited-edition model were made.

sporting than the Chevrolet, had a powerful image. Building on that image, Ford took the Thunderbird into a rather different market in the later 1950s and early 1960s, returning to the car's original market in 1964 with the good-looking new Mustang. Inevitably, convertible versions figured strongly in the range and, just as inevitably, Chevrolet hit back with its Camaro in both closed and open forms.

Alongside the full-sized convertibles in the early 1960s, there were also convertible versions of the 'compact' sedans. However, the compacts were short-lived, and by the middle of the 1960s the American public was once again demanding large cars. This preference was reinforced by new safety and exhaust-emissions standards which became Federal law in 1968: it was easier to engineer passenger protection into larger cars, and as emissions-control equipment sapped engine power, so engine sizes went up in order to maintain performance.

The impact of government legislation on America's domestic motor manufacturers was dramatic and far-reaching. Further legislation followed that of 1968, tightening up both safety and emissions standards, and then in 1973 came additional measures introducing fuel-economy standards as well. The inevitable result of all these restrictions placed on the manufacturers was that the typical American car shrank in size during the early 1970s. New convertibles in this period were few and far between, however. The mass of safety legislation had led to fears that open cars would eventually be banned in America on safety grounds, and the country's motor manufacturers were understandably reluctant to risk investment in developing and tooling up for new convertibles in case legislation made these unsaleable. Chevrolet stopped building convertible Corvettes in 1975, and the last full-sized open car of the decade was built by Cadillac in 1976. Only the specialist, low-volume manufacturers like Excalibur continued to build open cars for the rest of the 1970s.

These pages: The typical American convertible of the middle and later 1950s was not substantially different from its forebears. The styling of the 1957 Chevrolet Bel Air (left) and the 1958 Cadillac Eldorado Biarritz (below) followed the longer/lower/wider trend of the times, however, and both horsepower and engine sizes were up: the Chevrolet had a 283 cubic-inch V8, with anywhere from 185 to 283bhp depending on options, and the Cadillac's 365 cubic-inch V8 put out 365bhp. The Ford Thunderbird (right) was an attempt at something new, however, for it added a touch of luxury and practicality to the two-door open car. The 1956 model illustrated probably had a 312 cubic-inch V8 with between 215 and 225bhp.

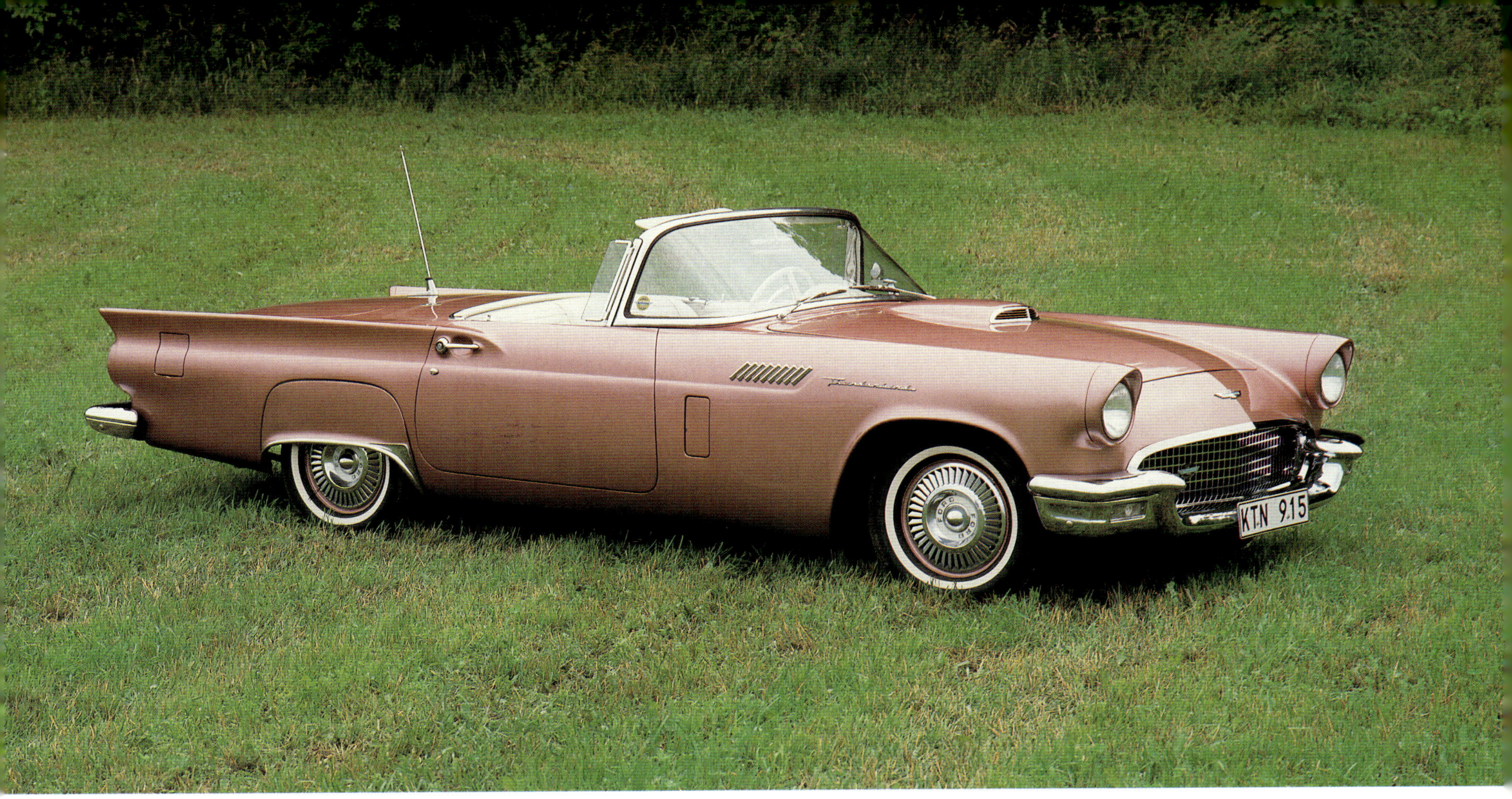
KTN 915

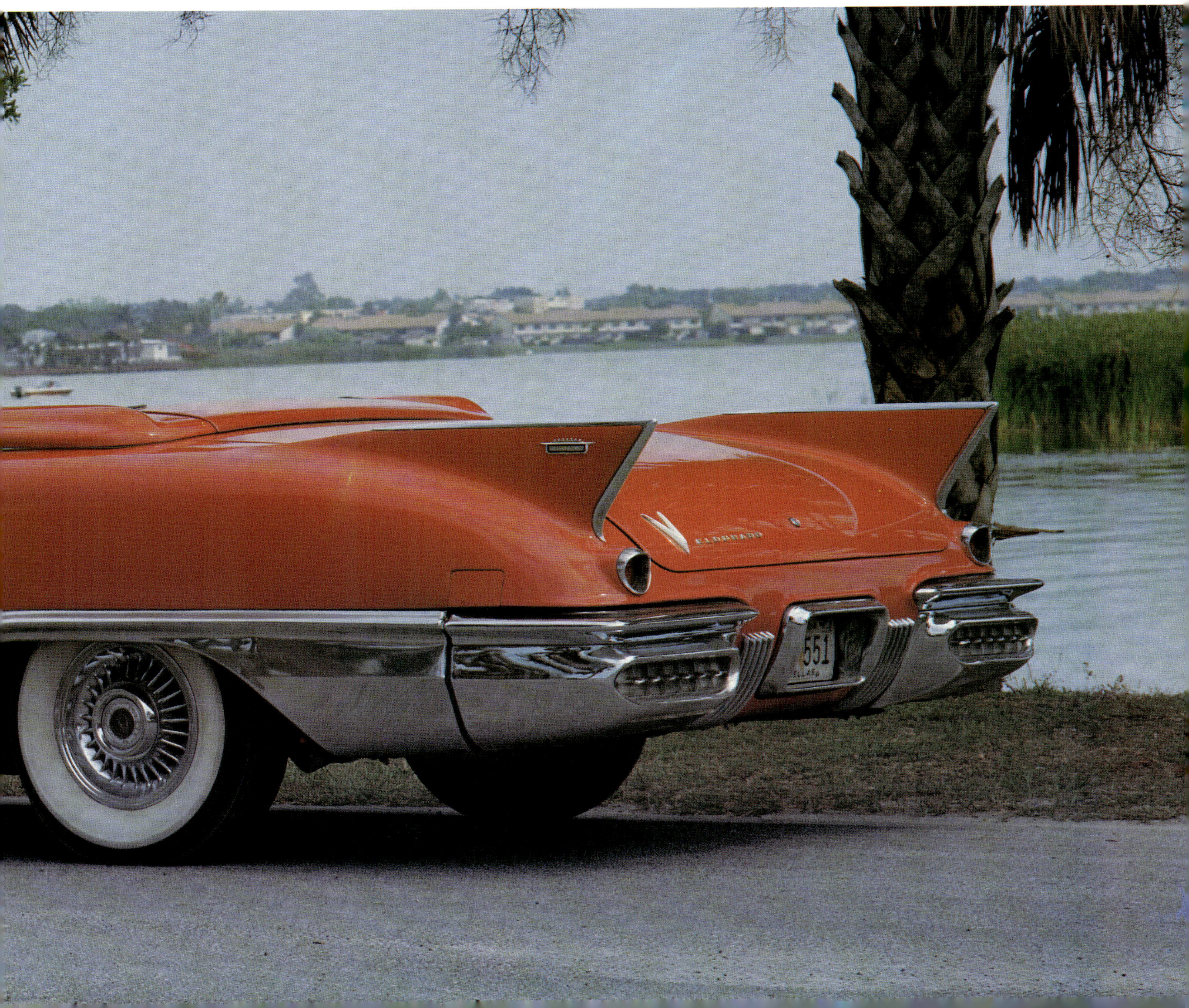

Nevertheless, no safety legislation was ever introduced to ban the sale of open cars in the United States. In the early 1980s, domestic manufacturers reintroduced convertibles to their ranges, although the first ones to appear were actually converted from closed cars by smaller companies under contract to the big manufacturers: that way it would have been less costly to pull out of the whole operation if sales were poor. In fact, sales *were* slow at first and, even though they picked up later, by the end of the 1980s it seemed as if the American public had lost the habit of buying open cars.

The 'Mainstream' Convertible

The story of the mainstream American convertible essentially follows that of the American sedan. All the major manufacturers had convertible versions of their main models in the 1940s, 1950s, 1960s, and early 1970s, and in general the styling of these cars reflected that of the parent sedans. The convertible was as often as not derived from the two-door hard-top model – the hard top being essentially a pillarless coupe, a type which first became popular in the United States during the early 1950s. Most of the large American convertibles were therefore two-door models, although there were exceptions. One such was the luxurious Lincoln Continental, which was available as a four-door convertible between 1961 and 1965.

Ford, the maker of the Lincoln, also bucked the trend in the late 1950s with the ambitious Fairlane 500 Skyliner retractable hard top. This car represented an intriguing new approach to the large convertible in America, for its metal hard-top-style roof could be automatically retracted into the trunk to create an open car. (Interestingly, Peugeot in France had built such cars in small numbers during the 1930s.) Sadly, the car's cost and the impracticality of its rear-hinged trunk killed off this model within three years, and it was not followed up.

There was one further aberration: the major American manufacturers introduced 'compact' sedans in around 1960 to cash in on the market for smaller cars which the European imports – mainly Volkswagen Beetles – had created in the late 1950s, and convertible versions followed a few years later. The main contenders were Chevrolet's 1962 Corvair, Plymouth's 1963 Valiant, and Ford's 1963 Falcon, but all were short-lived. By the mid-1960s, the American public had demonstrated its preference for larger cars, and the compacts and their convertible derivatives faded away. The large con-

Above: The 1959 Cadillac models had the tallest tail fins in the business, but that was only part of their new and sleeker styling. The engines were 390 cubic-inch V8s, which offered very good performance, although handling was sacrificed to the American taste for a soft boulevard ride.

Above right: This 1959 Ford Galaxie Skyliner is from the last season of the retractable hard-top model's production. Previous retractables – for 1957 and 1958 – had been designated Fairlane 500 Skyliner models. The standard engine in 1959's cars was a 200bhp, 292 cubic-inch V8, but larger V8s of up to 300bhp could also be had.

Right: The styling details of the 1960 Plymouth Fury convertible were certainly distinctive, but underneath it all was a standard-sized American sedan with a 118-inch wheelbase and a powerful V8 engine.

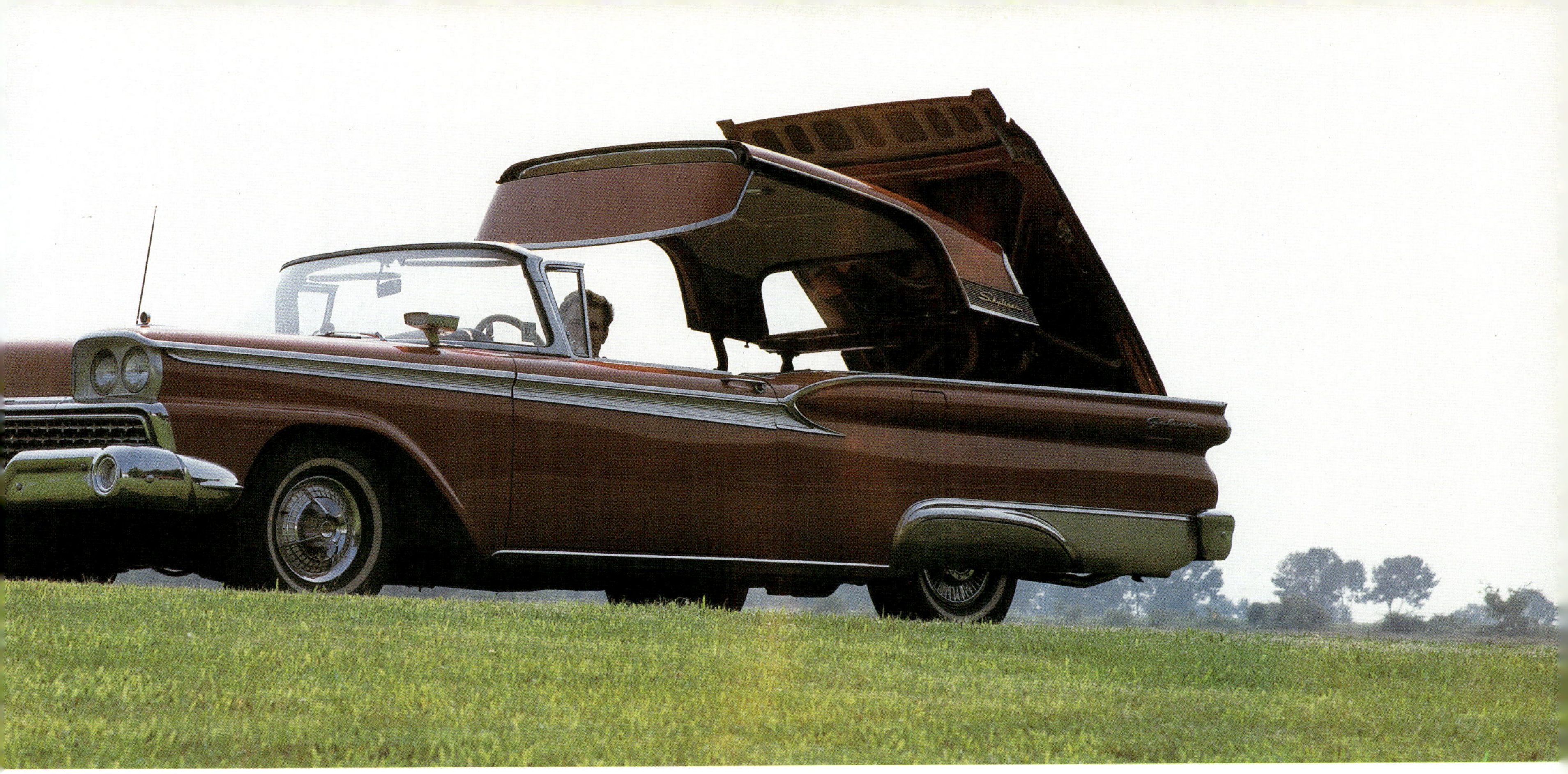

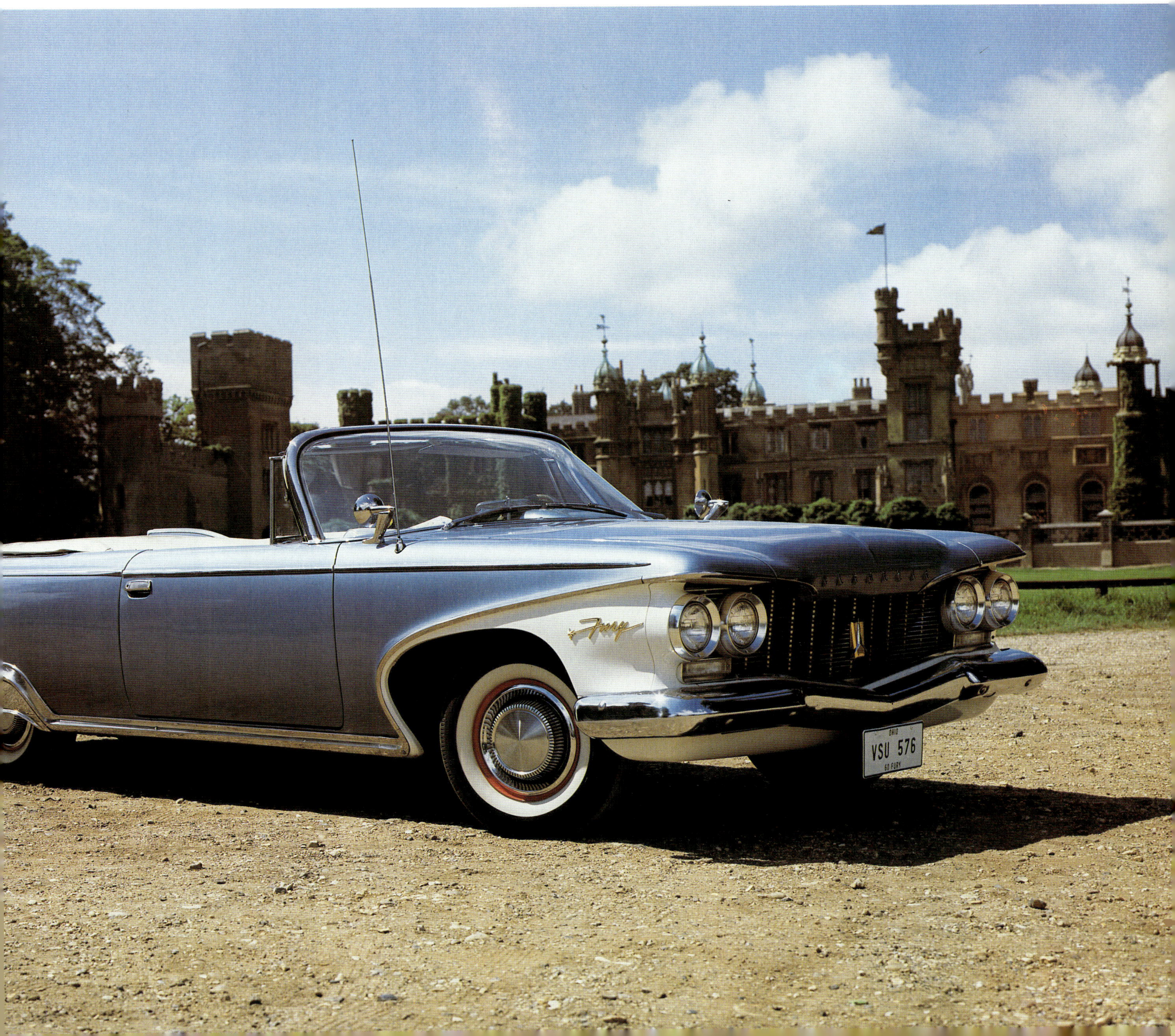
VSU 576

vertible reigned supreme for the rest of the 1960s, but its future looked increasingly doubtful as the decade drew to a close. Some manufacturers dropped convertible models early in the 1970s, and the last large convertible in production during that decade was Cadillac's Eldorado, which survived until 1976.

The convertible based on a coupe or sedan did not return until 1981 and, when it did, it was no longer 'large' — the downsizing of the 1970s had seen to that. Buick, Chrysler and Dodge announced new convertible models for 1982, but sales were slow. Buick pulled out after four years, and Dodge only lasted a year longer, although it returned with the new Shadow convertible in 1990. Gradually, other manufacturers added convertibles to their ranges: Chevrolet and Pontiac did so in 1983 and Cadillac in 1984; AMC followed suit in 1985 (with the Alliance, based on a small French Renault sedan); while Oldsmobile waited until 1989.

The 1980s American convertible was very different from its pre-1970s equivalent, however. It was often based on the smallest model in the range or on the next one up the ladder. Mostly, the larger models (themselves much smaller than in previous times) had no convertible versions. Sales of these new small convertibles were encouraging, but not great enough for manufacturers to risk more than one convertible body at a time. So far, there is no indication that the 1990s will be any different.

The Open Sportscar

The American open sportscar is very different from the European type. Until Chevrolet's Corvette of 1953, no such model was built by an American manufacturer; and few cars built subsequently even tried to capture the Corvette's market. The 1954 Kaiser-Darrin roadster was perhaps a serious attempt, even aping the Chevrolet's use of fiberglass body-construction, but it could not survive its manufacturer's financial problems and quickly disappeared.

These pages: As America entered the 1960s, the full-sized convertible was still intact. Representative of the full-sized luxury models are the 1961 Cadillac (left) with its 325bhp, 390 cubic-inch V8 engine, and the Lincoln Continental (right) from the same year. The Lincoln was particularly noteworthy for its four-door convertible bodywork, which was rigid only because of reinforcements which added enormous weight: it needed its 300bhp V8 engine. The compacts were already on the market, however. The Chevrolet Corvair (below), with its rear-mounted flat-six engine of just 80bhp, had been announced for 1960 and convertibles had arrived for 1962. Known as Monza spyder models, these had 150bhp versions of the flat-six.

88 CLASSIC CONVERTIBLES

The Corvette was always much bigger than the European sportscars, and was almost always more potent than most of them. Handling and road-holding, however, were not always up to the best European standards. Forty years on, the Corvette name is still the one most popularly associated with open sportscars in America, although not all Corvettes have been convertibles and, in fact, there was no convertible Corvette between 1975 and 1986. The Corvette has gone through six generations, with major new types being introduced in 1956, 1958, 1963, 1968 and 1984; but it was symptomatic of the slow market for convertibles in the 1980s that the sixth-generation cars had been on sale for two years before open versions became available.

If the Corvette was not challenged directly by the major American manufacturers, its market was nevertheless obliquely attacked, and primarily by Ford. The 1955 Thunderbird was Ford's first attempt at a two-seater sportscar, although it was less overtly sporty than the Corvette and more luxurious and practical. Ford, in fact, marketed it as a 'personal car' rather than as a sportscar, and within three years had followed the implications of that description, taking the Thunderbird into a different market, where it put on weight and lost whatever sporting pretensions it once had. So convincingly did hard-top coupe versions outsell the convertibles that the last open Thunderbird was built in 1966.

Meanwhile, the Thunderbird's original place in the market had been taken in 1964 by the Ford Mustang, again an obviously sporting machine, and one which was launched into the 'muscle-car' era, with its emphasis on power

Above: The Ford Mustang arrived in 1964 and rapidly became an American institution. The favorite engine option in early cars like this one was a 210bhp 289 cubic-inch V8. Coupes, convertibles and fastbacks all figured in the range of body styles.

Above right: By the later 1960s, the compacts had gone, but their legacy remained: this 1970 Dodge Challenger had a wheelbase just two inches longer than a Chevrolet Corvair's. The muscle-car era had also left its mark, however, and the engines in most examples were once again large and powerful V8s.

Right: The American convertible was a dying breed by the time this Oldsmobile 4-4-2 was built in 1971. Only 1304 examples were sold that year, all with a 455 cubic-inch V8, which put out 340bhp.

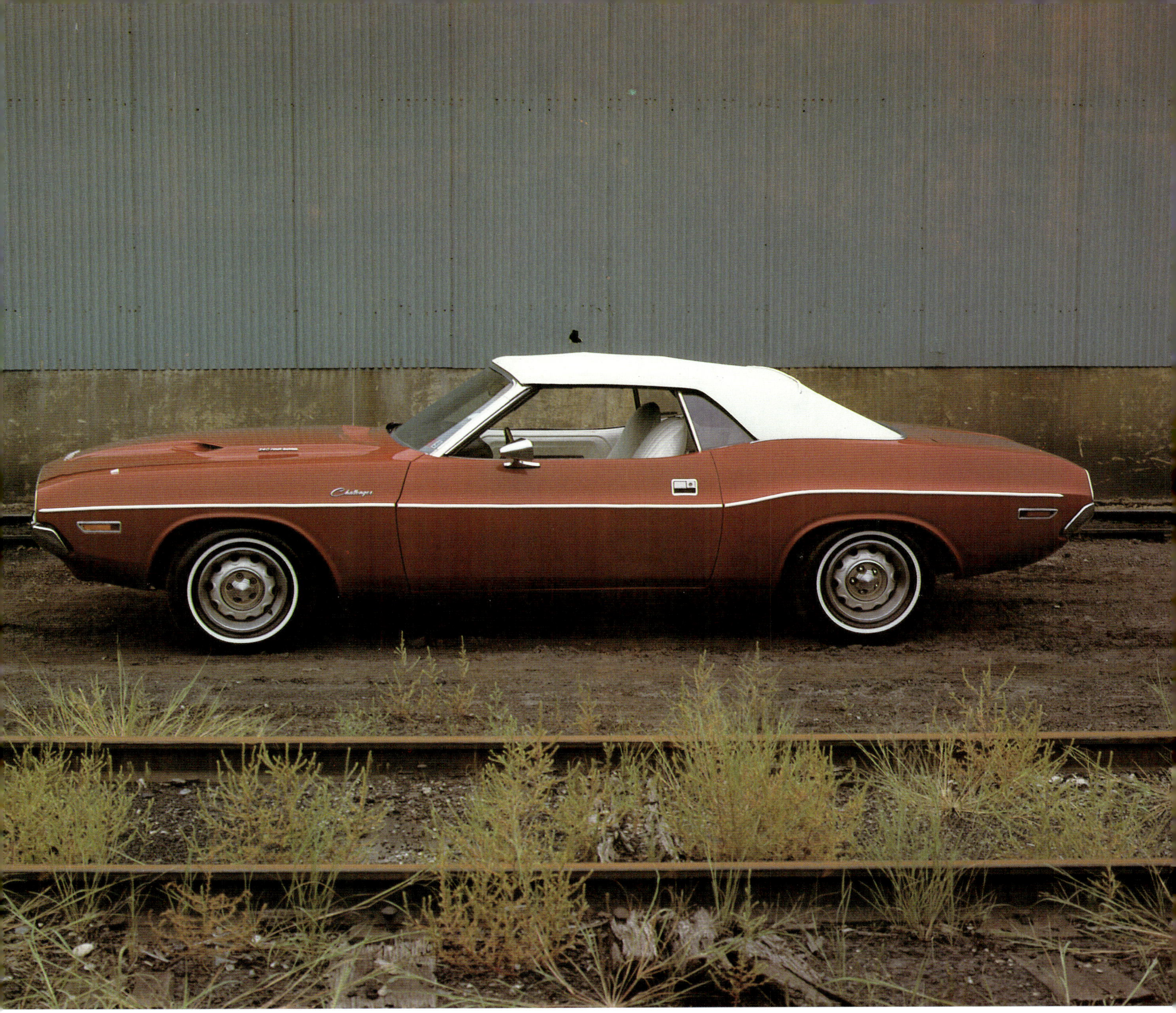

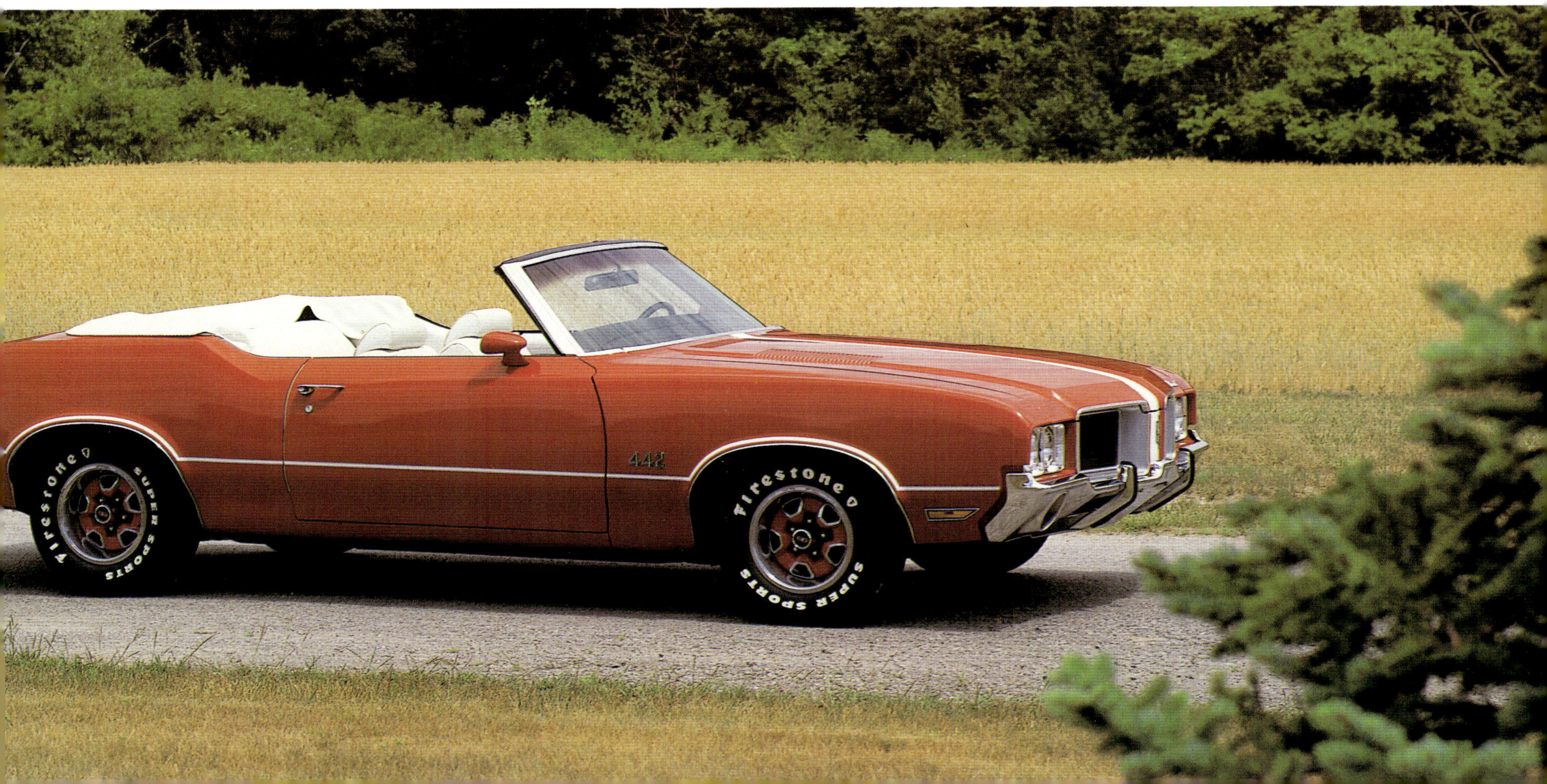
Firestone
SUPER SPORTS
4·4·2

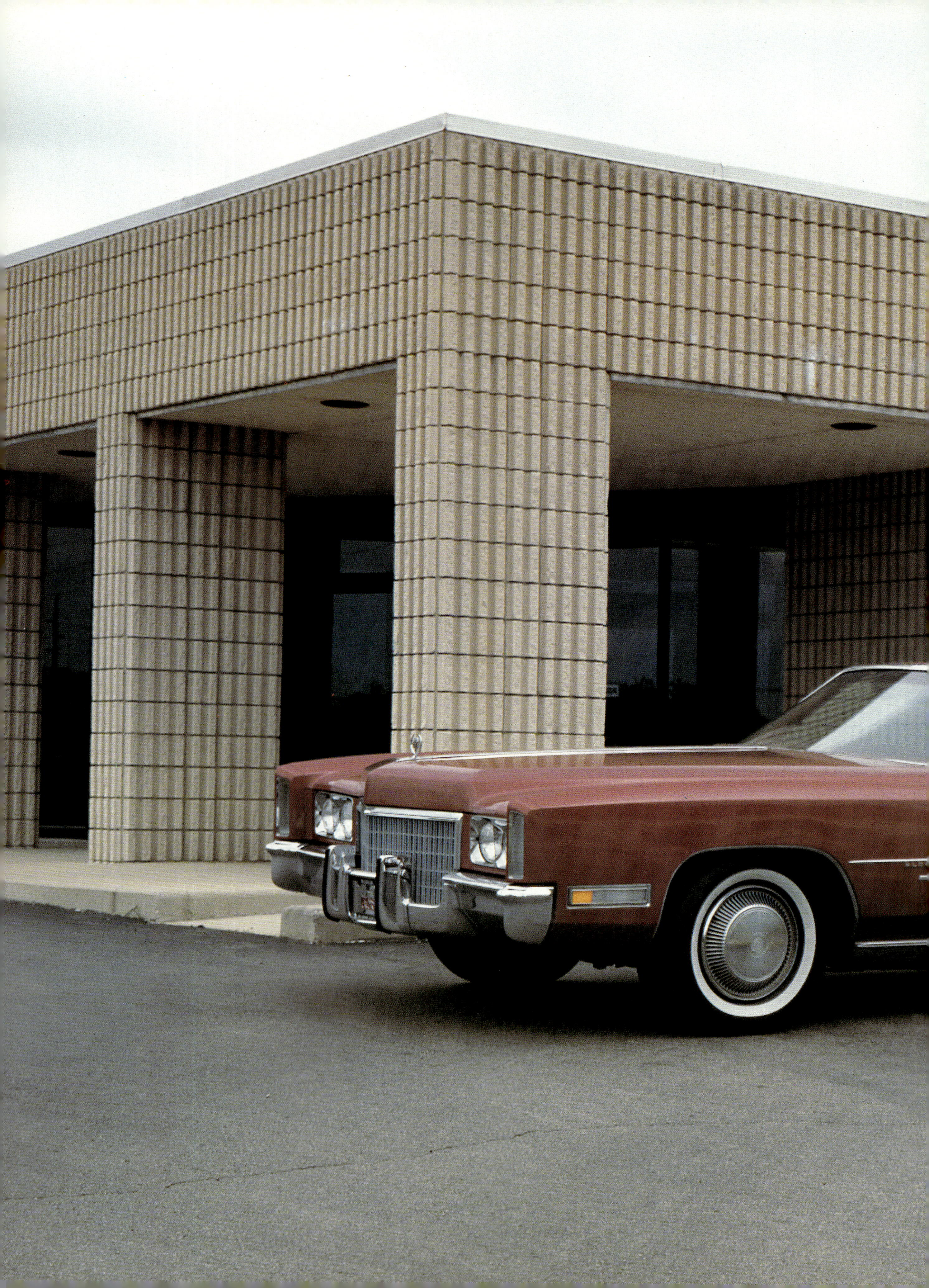

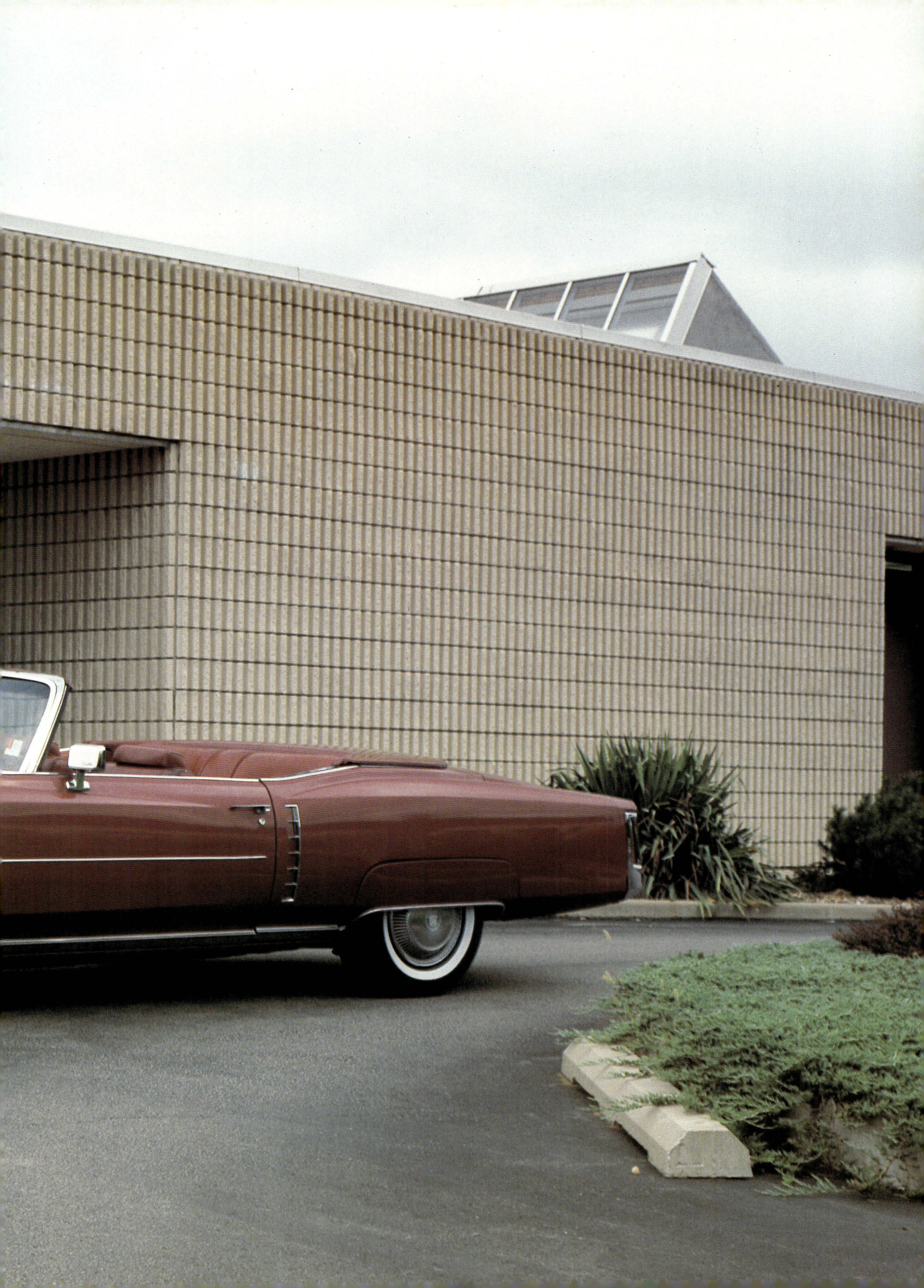

92 CLASSIC CONVERTIBLES

Previous pages: Emissions-control gear began to stifle the big V8s in the early 1970s. This 1972 Cadillac Eldorado convertible maintained all the luxurious traditions associated with the marque, but its 500 cubic-inch engine put out a miserable 235bhp. In pre-emissions-control days, there had been one horsepower per cubic inch.

Top left: Open versions of Chevrolet's first-generation Camaro, available between 1967 and 1969, had either straight-six or V8 engines. Fears of legislation banning open cars ensured that no convertible version of the second-generation Camaros was ever made.

Left: An open Camaro became available again for 1987. This is the IROC-Z model, which came as standard with a 215bhp V8 of 305 cubic inches, and could be ordered with the optional 225bhp, 350 cubic-inch motor. The clean-cut, chiseled lines were quite different from those of earlier Camaros.

Below: Corvette customers were treated to an open model in 1986 – a year before the open Camaro returned. Again, the lines were finely chiseled. The only engine available was the 350 cubic-inch V8 which, in this application, gave 230bhp.

Above right: Cadillac tried very hard with the Allanté, but even Pininfarina styling and a 200bhp V8 could not guarantee big sales volumes. Build quality was not always all it might have been, which did not help this luxury two-seater to make an impression on the market.

Right: Refinement rather than performance was the name of the game at Excalibur, which fitted a 305 cubic-inch V8 with just 155bhp to this Series V Phaeton. These exclusive and expensive retrocars were sold in only small numbers, and in 1986 – the year this example was built – Excalibur filed for bankruptcy.

and performance. The car was a sensational success, although sales dropped during 1975 after the first year of a downsized, less powerful, convertible-free Mustang II range. Targa-top Mustangs reappeared before the 1970s were over, and gave the range open models once again, but proper convertible versions did not reappear until 1983. The Mustang remains popular in the United States, where its main challenger has been Chevrolet's Camaro, introduced for 1967 but available in convertible form only between 1967 and 1969 and then again from 1987.

The most recent attempt by an American manufacturer to make an open two-seater is Cadillac's Allanté, a luxurious sporting car introduced in 1986 in fixed-roof form as a competitor for the Mercedes-Benz SL models. The convertible version did not appear until 1989, but even this did not make the car into the success its makers had hoped for, and the Allanté was withdrawn in the early 1990s. Clearly, the convertible market in America has still not regained its former good health.

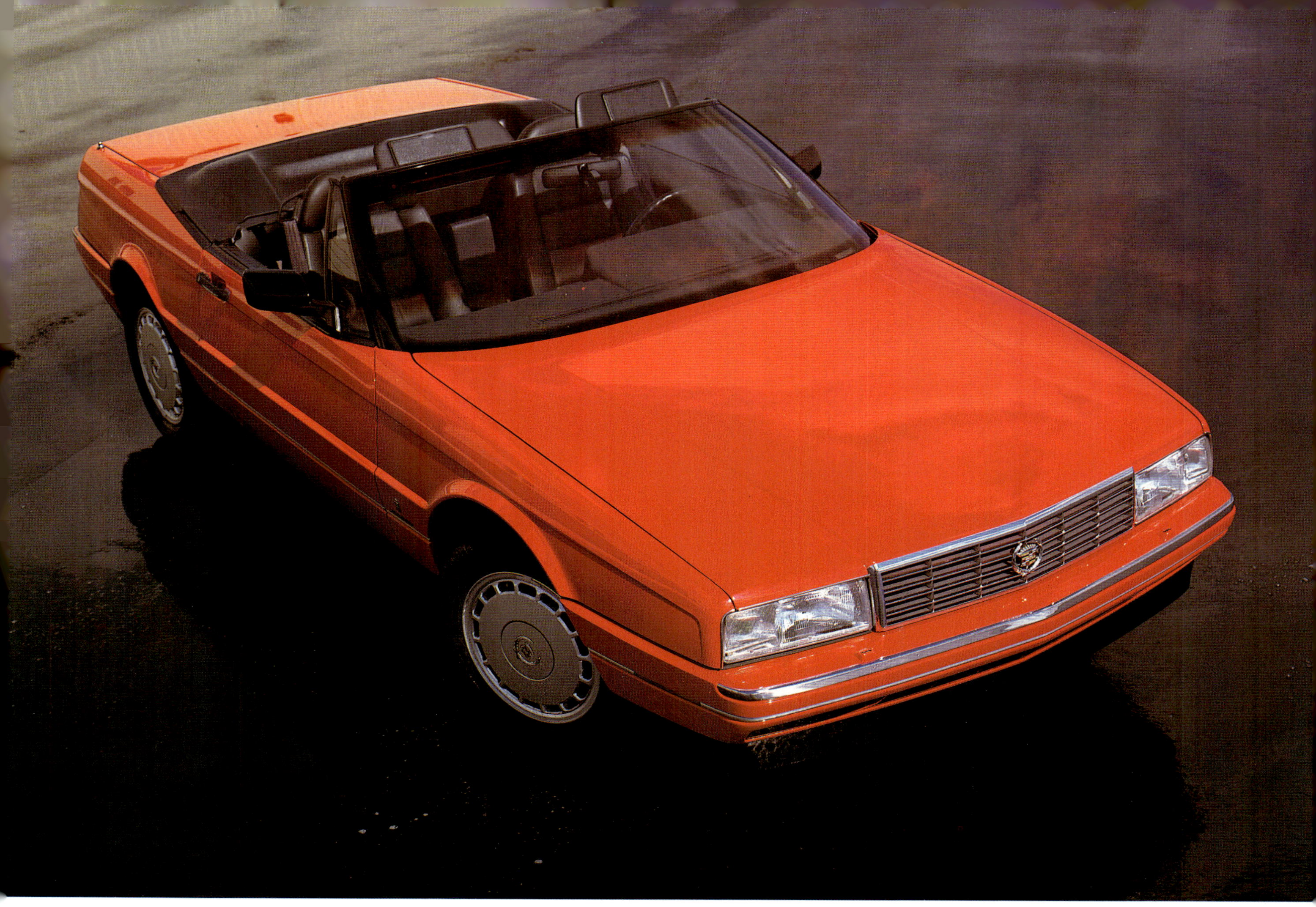

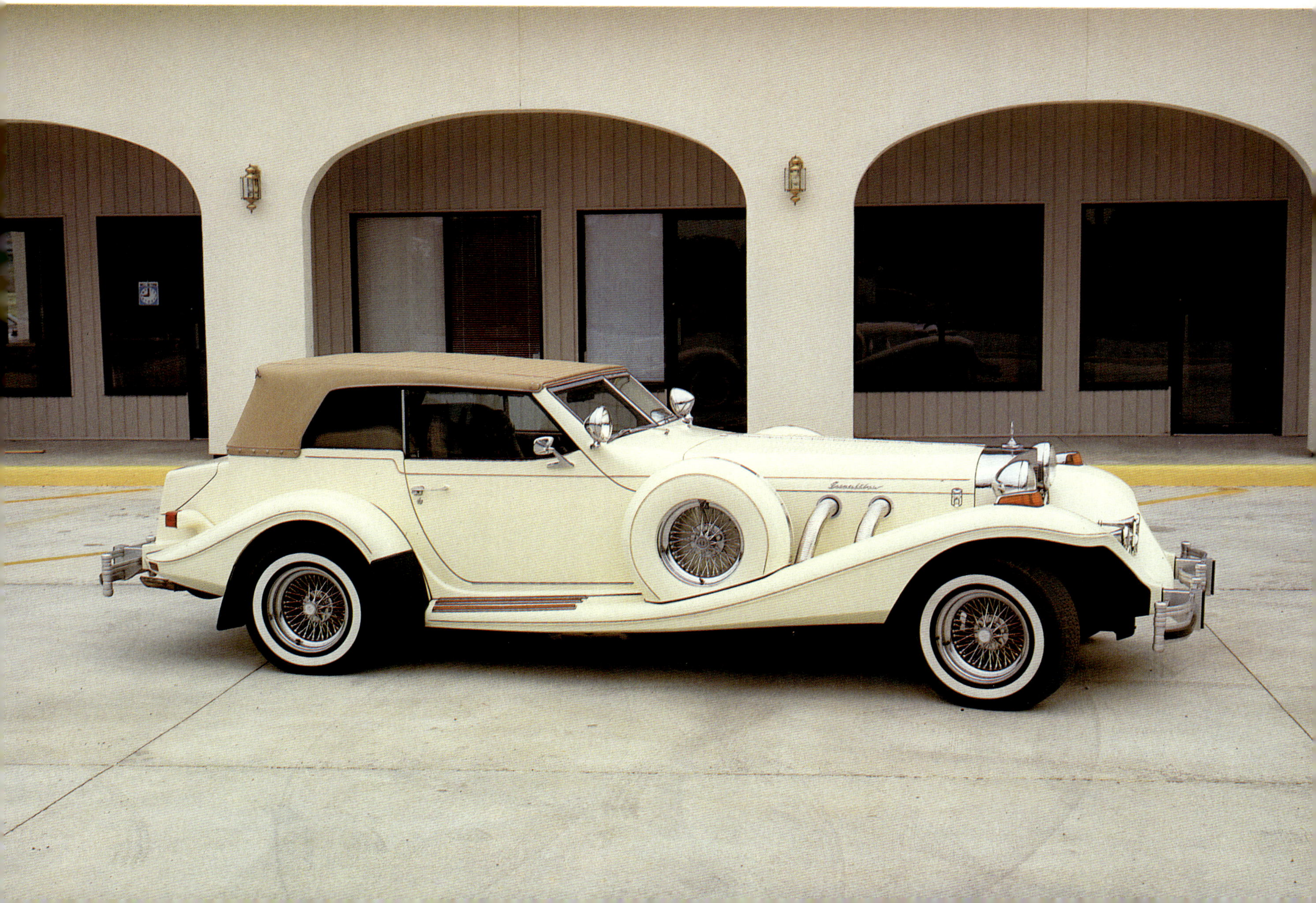

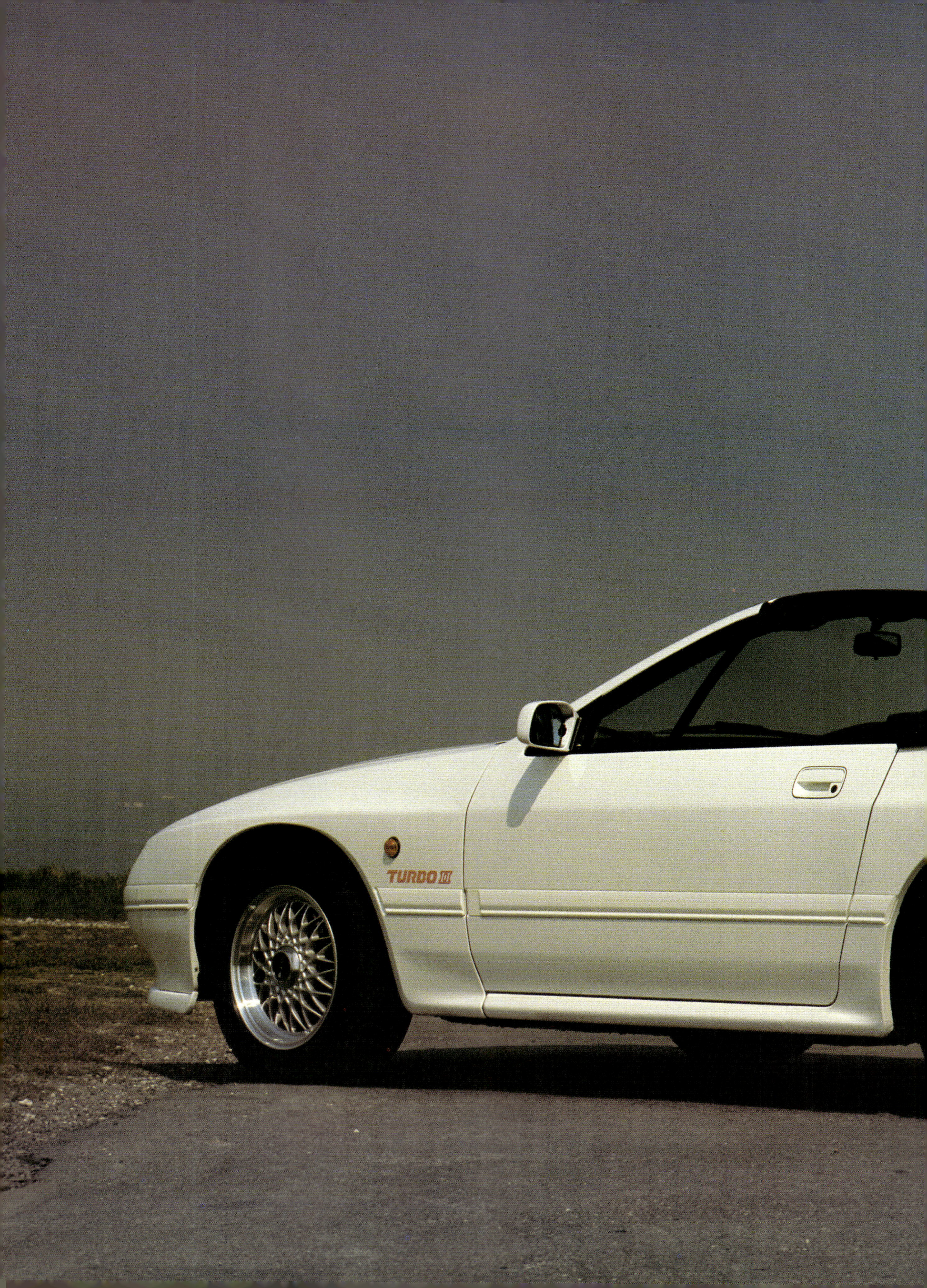
TURBO II

The Japanese Convertible

CLASSIC CONVERTIBLES

At the end of World War II Japan's relatively small car industry was put under American control, and the first years of peace were spent in building commercial vehicles which would help to put the country's economy back on its feet. Only limited production of private cars was permitted before 1949, and thereafter economic factors prevented a rapid increase in car-ownership in Japan.

Those who could afford cars often bought foreign imports, until government action in the mid-1950s restricted these and supported the creation of a Japanese private-car industry much greater than that which had existed in the 1930s. Lessons were learned from co-operative ventures with Western companies, and a number of British, American and French sedans were built under license in Japan. By the late 1950s the Japanese car industry was able to sever these relationships with the West, and during the 1960s it expanded enormously, aided by aggressive export policies and by protectionist policies in its home market. This expansion was even greater in the 1970s when, after the 1973 oil crisis, a demand arose for the relatively small and economical cars typical of Japanese manufacturers. Profits made in the 1970s enabled the Japanese car industry to innovate on a much greater scale than before, and to produce some exciting and technologically-advanced designs for the 1980s and 1990s.

Yet the convertible car was largely an irrelevance to the Japanese car industry before the 1980s. Small numbers of open runabouts were made for the home market in the 1950s, and there were some attempts at copying European two-seater sports models at the end of that decade and in the early 1960s. However, just as the major Japanese manufacturers were gearing themselves up for an onslaught on the international markets, the threat of American legislation banning open cars in that country began to loom. Only Nissan – then trading as Datsun – and Honda had tasted export success with a convertible model before the entire Japanese car industry began to focus on closed bodywork.

For convertibles, the 1970s were barren years, but the early 1980s saw a cautious return to open cars. That the Japanese manufacturers should have trodden much the same path as their American counterparts at that time was no surprise in view of Japan's determination to sell cars in the United States. First came open sports models, but by the end of the decade the Japanese manufacturers were also building intriguing open 'fun' cars; many of these had only limited availability outside Japan itself. Unlike Western manufacturers, the Japanese have not yet tackled the straightforward convertible sedan; but it would be reasonable to assume that they will do so if the market for such cars – particularly in the United States – starts to look profitable.

Previous pages: Among the most respected Japanese sportscars of the 1980s was the Mazda RX-7, seen here in 1987 cabriolet guise. The engine was a Wankel rotary type, which gave both high performance and refinement.

Above: One of the earliest Japanese convertibles was the 1959 Datsun S211, which was quite clearly inspired by European styling. With just 988cc, it was no performer.

Left: Datsun followed up with the SPL 310 in 1962, which was a very much better car, and sold well in the USA. The original 1500 model developed into a 1600, and finally into a 2000.

Right: Honda had already established its name as a motorcycle manufacturer, and adapted motorcycle technology to its cars in the 1960s. The S800 convertible offered good performance from its tiny 800cc engine, but Western customers found it hard to take such a small engine seriously. Pictured here is a 1967 model.

Overleaf: By the 1980s, Japanese sportscars were a force to be reckoned with. The Datsun 280ZX turbo, seen here in 1982 Targa-top guise, had a 2.8-liter straight-six engine and offered a very respectable performance. It went down well in the USA.

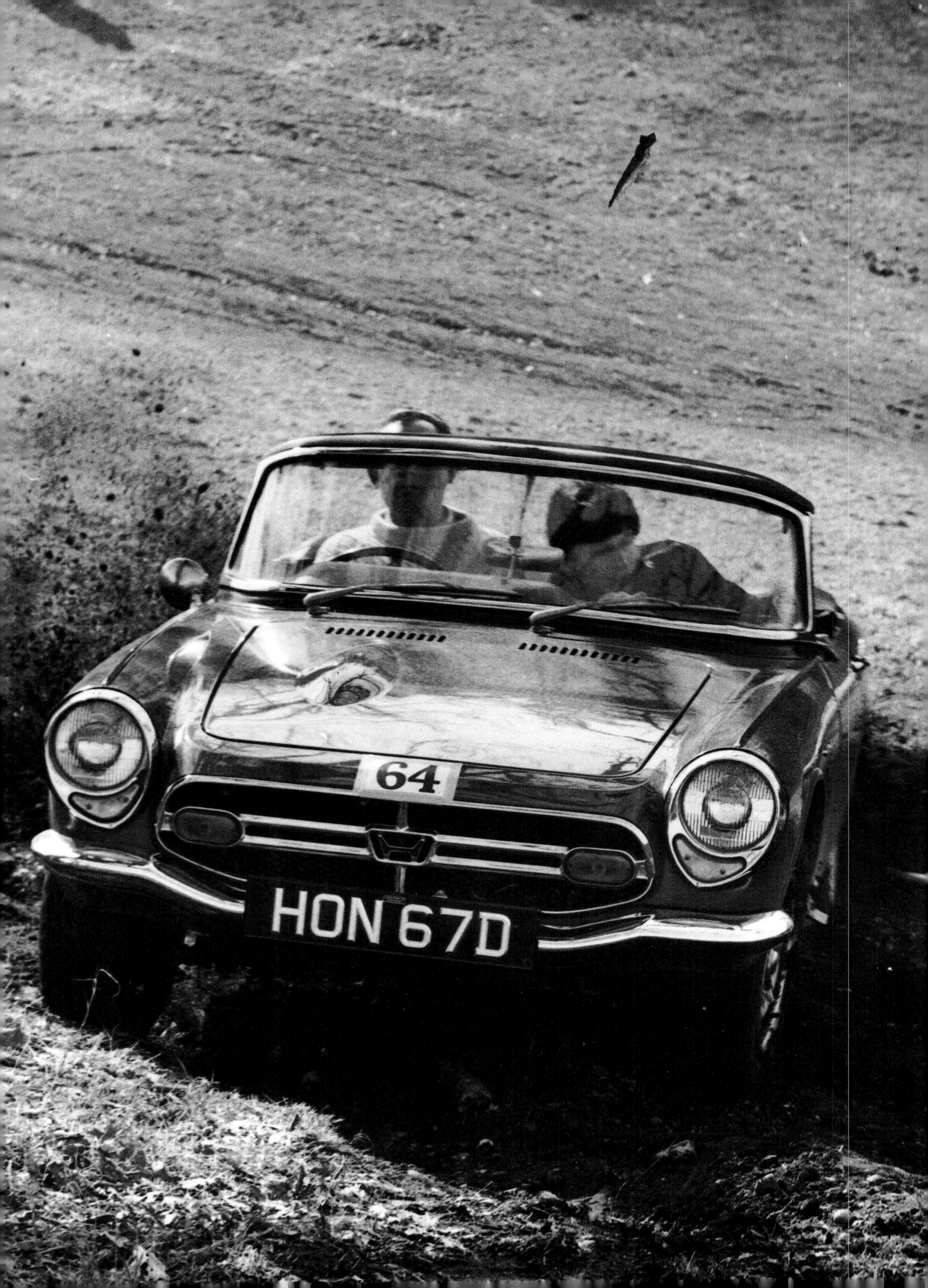
64
HON 67D

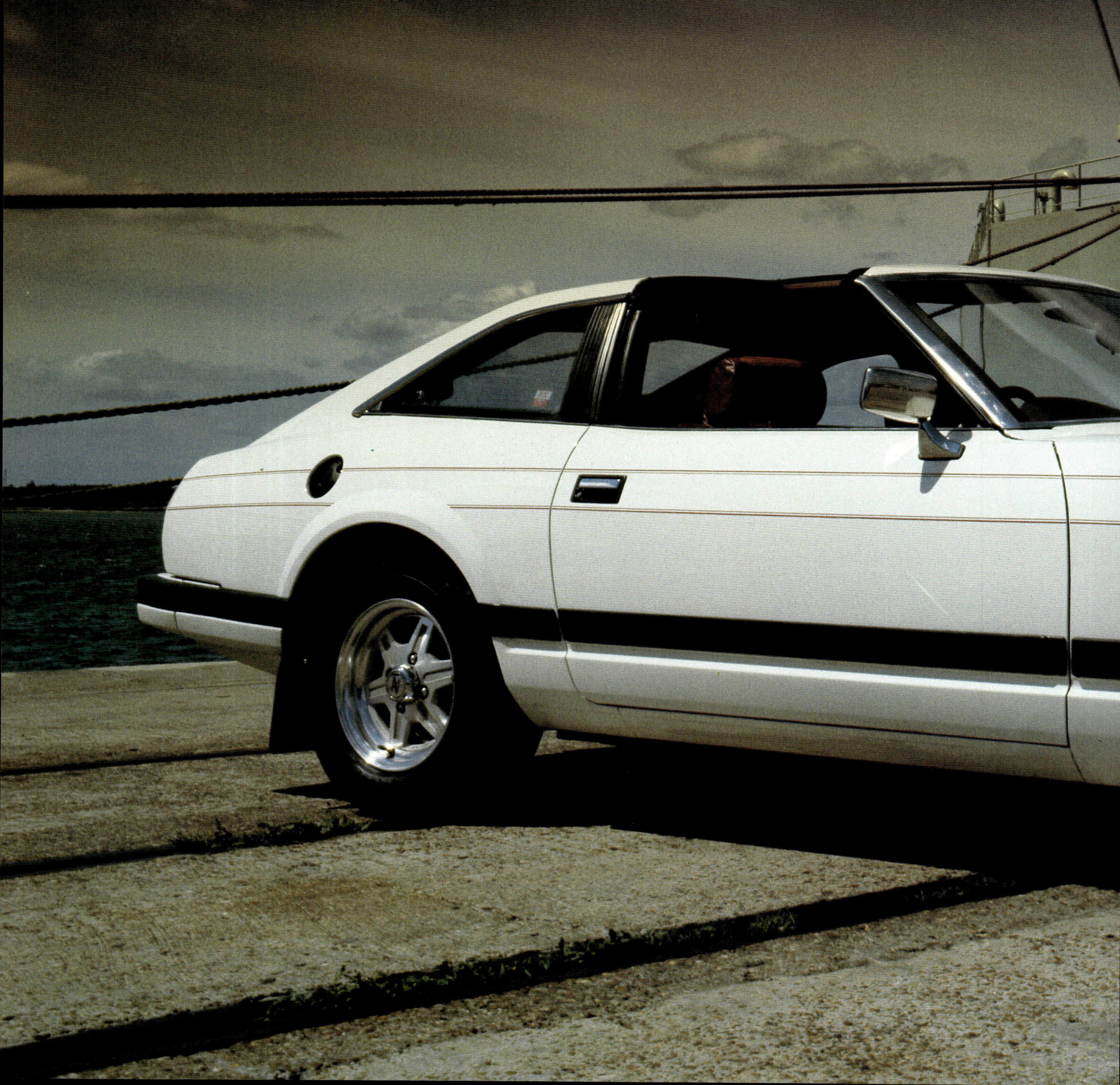

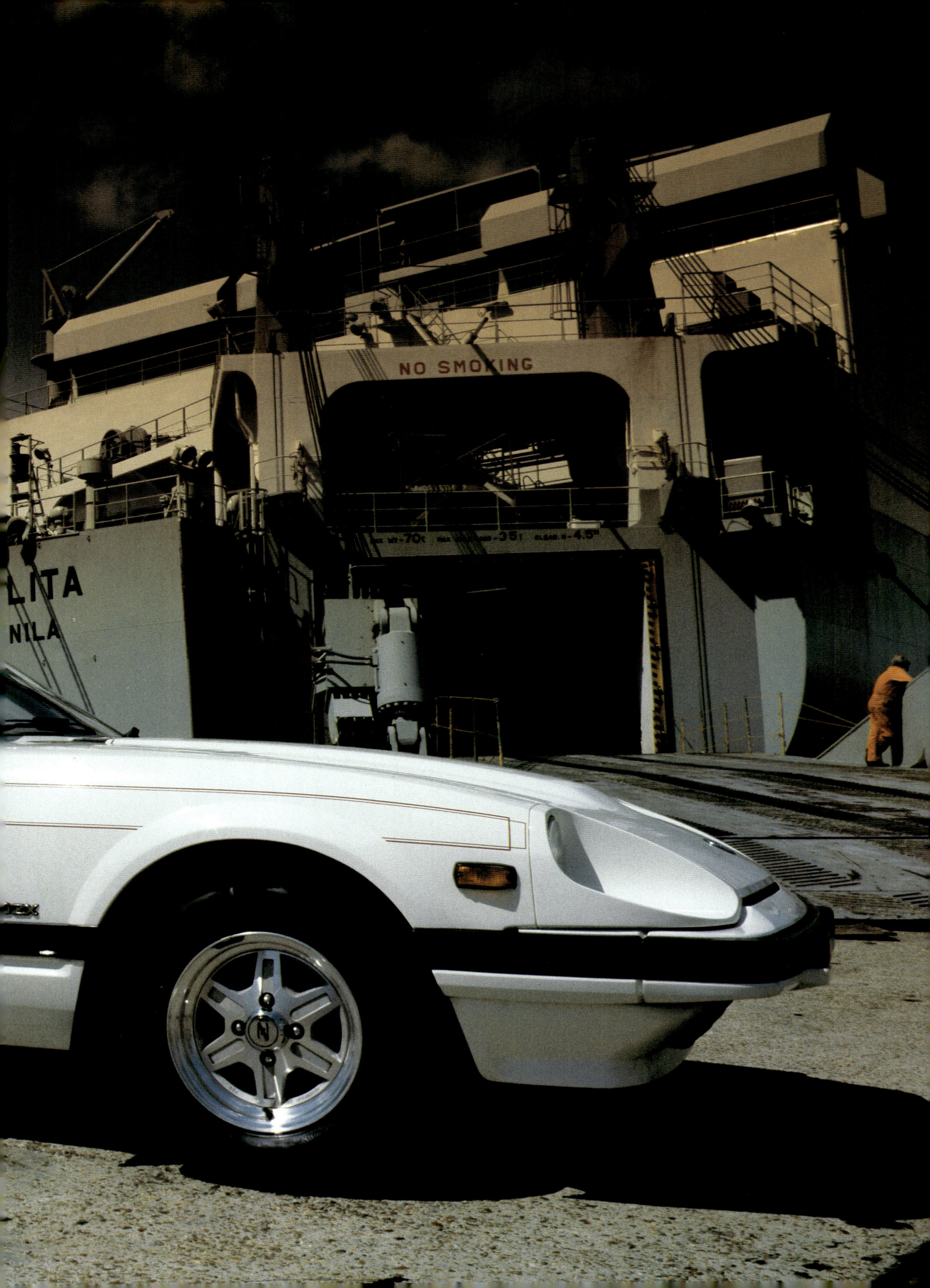
NO SMOKING
LITA
NILA

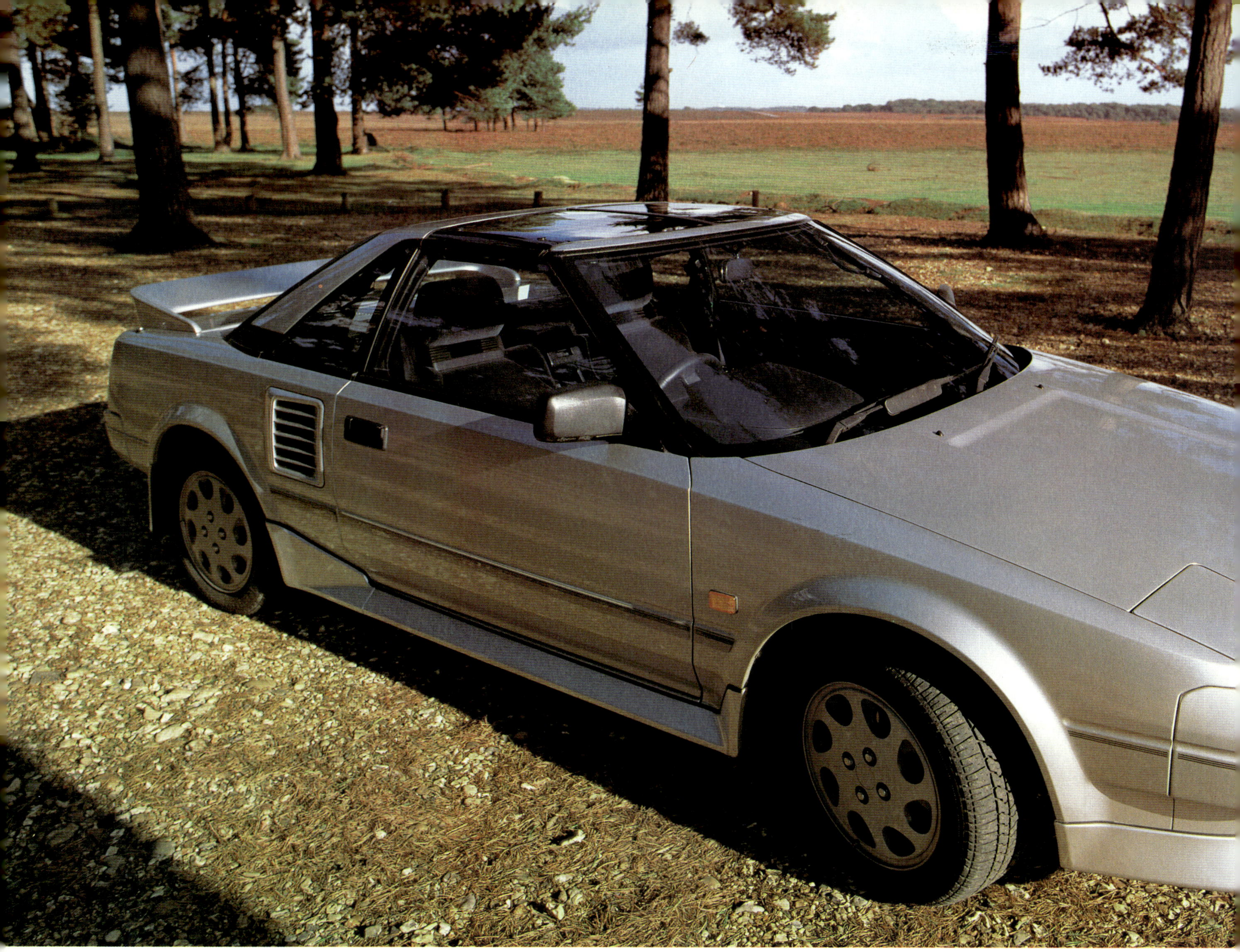

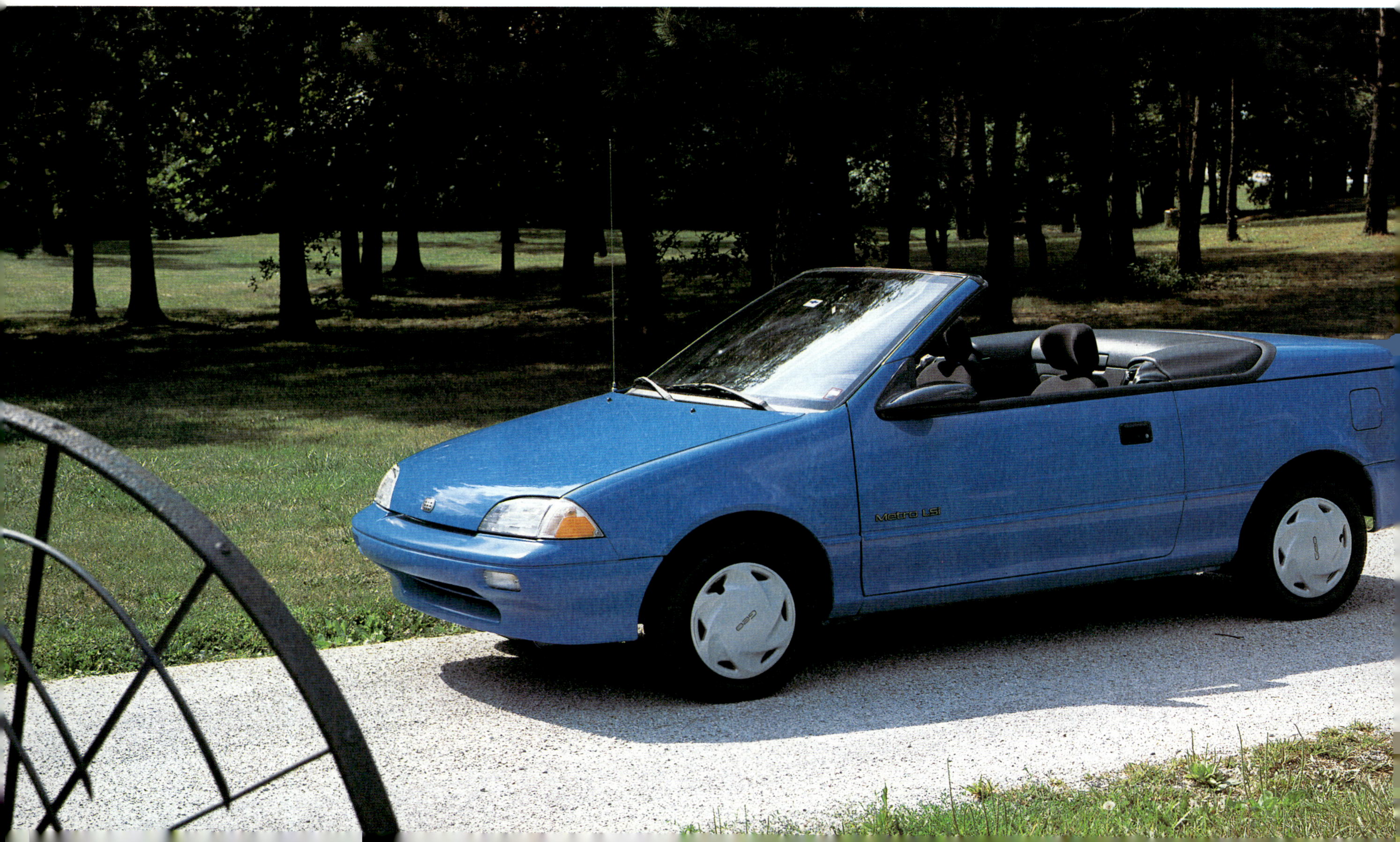

THE JAPANESE CONVERTIBLE 101

Top left: The Toyota MR2 of 1984 showed that the Japanese makers were prepared to exploit the gaps in the market left by the European makers. Building on the advances of the Fiat X1/9, this Targa-top, mid-engined sports two-seater commanded a great deal of respect.

Left: Sold under the Geo name in the USA, and to all appearances a product of GM's Chevrolet division, the 1-liter Metro was, in fact, a license-built Suzuki Cultus. From 1990, this stunning convertible version was available.

Above: Mazda never made any secret of the fact that its MX-5 was heavily based on the Lotus Elan of the 1960s. Nor could it deny that it was aimed at the US market, especially after it made its world première at the Chicago Show in 1989. The two-seater car has a 1598cc engine with 115bhp.

Small and Medium Sportscars in the 1950s and 1960s

It was Japan's motor-taxation policies which led to its motor industry's emphasis on small cars from the mid-1950s. Cars with engines of 360cc or less were subject to much reduced rates of tax, and their good fuel economy made them considerably cheaper to run than larger cars. These factors made them attractive to younger and less well-off buyers, but few manufacturers saw in this an opportunity to create open runabouts with youth appeal, because the domestic market was simply not large enough. Mikasa created such a car in the late 1950s, but the company's demise in 1961 did not encourage other manufacturers to take up the theme.

Even so, a number of the larger manufacturers introduced open two-seater sportscars in the early 1960s, all in the taxation class above the 360cc microcars. Datsun's first effort actually appeared in 1959 as the Fairlady S211 Sport, a rather bloated-looking vehicle whose designers had clearly examined the large Austin-Healeys for inspiration; but an altogether more significant design was announced in 1962. This was the SPL 310, a 1.5-liter two-seater which borrowed styling elements from MG and Fiat and was surprisingly competitive in relation to the established products in its market sector. It grew into a 1600 sportscar in 1965, and a 2000 in 1967 and, by the time production ceased in 1971, nearly 40,000 examples had been sold in the United States alone.

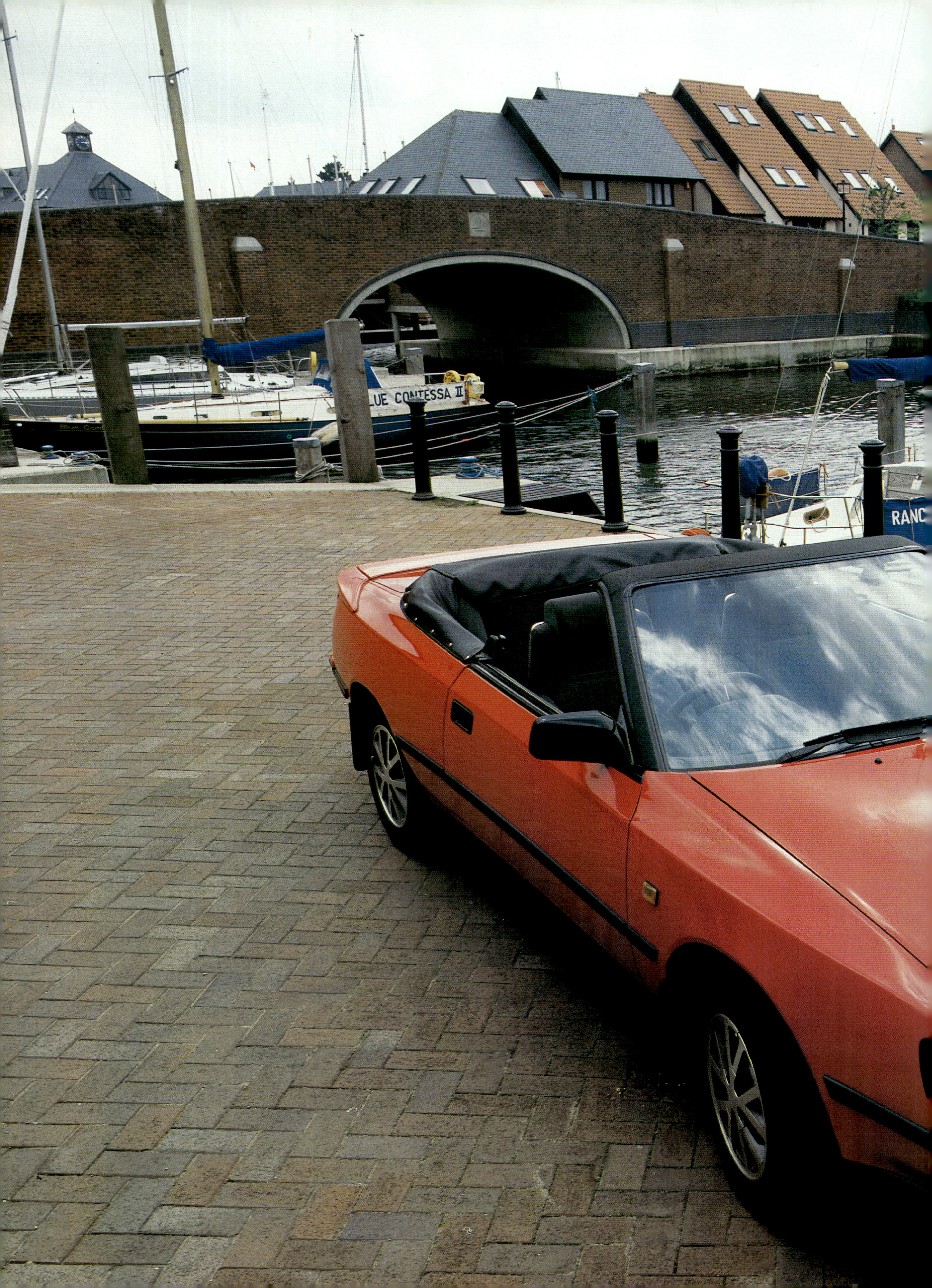
LUE CONTESSA II
RANC

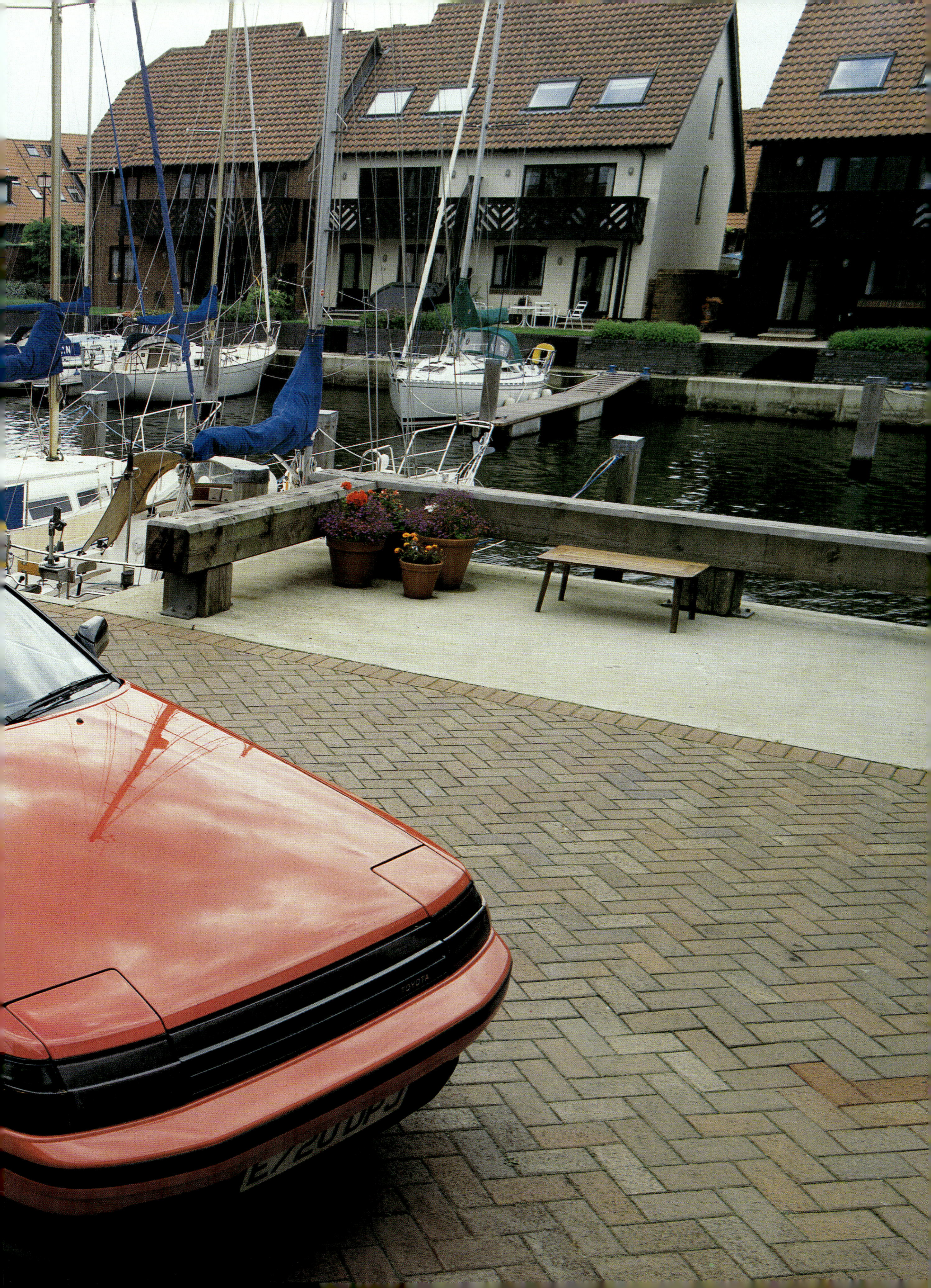

CLASSIC CONVERTIBLES

THE JAPANESE CONVERTIBLE 105

Previous pages: One of the most attractive cars to come out of Japan in the 1980s was the Toyota Celica cabriolet. The 2-liter four-cylinder engine delivered a 130mph performance.

Left: Convertible bodywork was also available on small four-wheel-drive leisure vehicles like Suzuki's stylish Vitara. The engine in this 1992 model was an injected 1590cc four-cylinder.

Right: The Nissan Figaro convertible was a retrocar made in a limited edition of 20,000 and available only in Japan. It had a sliding soft top which retracted into the trunk together with the rear window. The turbocharged 1-liter four-cylinder engine drove through an automatic transmission.

Below left: The Daihatsu Sportrak — known in some markets as a Rocky or a Feroza — was another example of a small four-wheel-drive vehicle with a removable canvas top. Passengers were protected by the rollover bar, clearly visible in this picture of an early 1990s model.

Below right: Honda's 1992 CRX, with its retractable roof panel.

Other important models came from Honda, which used motorcycle technology in its small S500 sportscar of 1962. This later grew into an S600 and finally an S800, and continued in production until 1969. Although it was never a best seller, it was technically quite a remarkable little car, and it helped to establish the name of Honda as a force to be reckoned with in the car markets outside Japan. The early 1960s also saw Toyota introduce a convertible version of its 1.5-liter 1000 economy sedan, while Daihatsu had a 797cc convertible among its first series-production models in 1963. However, neither car ever had much significance outside the Japanese home market.

Sports Convertibles in the 1980s and 1990s

Since returning to the open sportscar market in the early 1980s, the Japanese manufacturers have shown a marked preference for Targa-top models rather than full convertibles. No doubt the reason is the state of the convertible market in the United States, where Japanese manufacturers aim to sell a very large proportion of their sportscars: so far, the full convertible in the United States has proved less popular than the Targa-top car.

The first to offer an open sportscar model in the 1980s was Nissan, whose 280ZX 2+2 was offered in both closed-coupe and Targa-top forms as early as 1981. The car was successful enough for Nissan to standardize a Targa roof on its 1990 replacement, the 300ZX. Targa tops also featured on other Nissan sportscar models in the 1980s, such as the Pulsar NX and the later 100NX. Toyota and Honda were more cautious with Targa roofs, however, and the former's remarkable MR2 of 1984 did not acquire a Targa-top option until 1987, while Honda's CRX was always a coupe until the 1992 models were supplied with an electrically-retractable roof center section.

Real convertibles did exist, but were few and far between. Toyota's 1985 Celica looked superb without the metal roof of its coupe equivalent, but sales were insufficient to justify a convertible version of its 1989 successor.

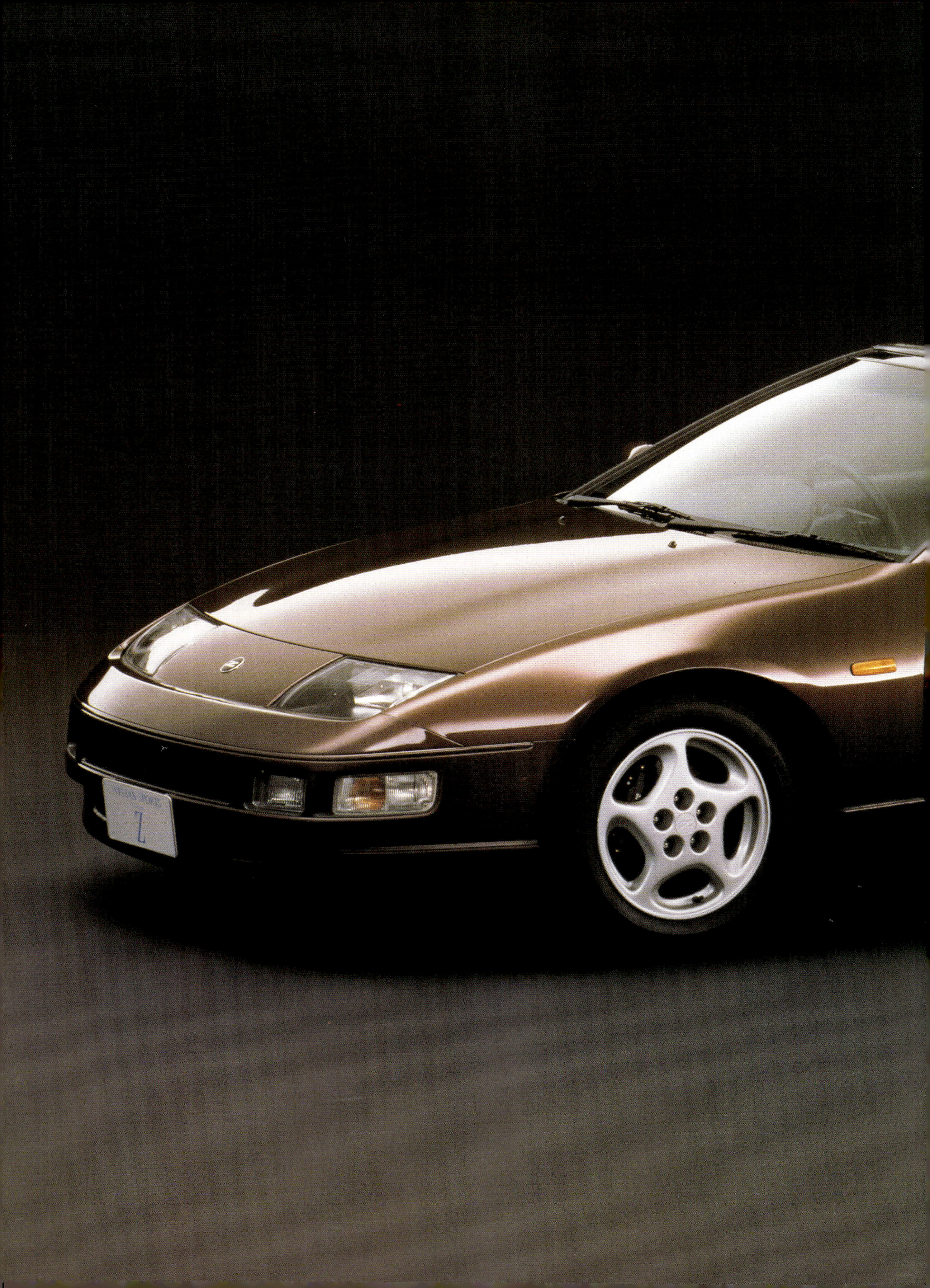
NISSAN SPORTS
Z

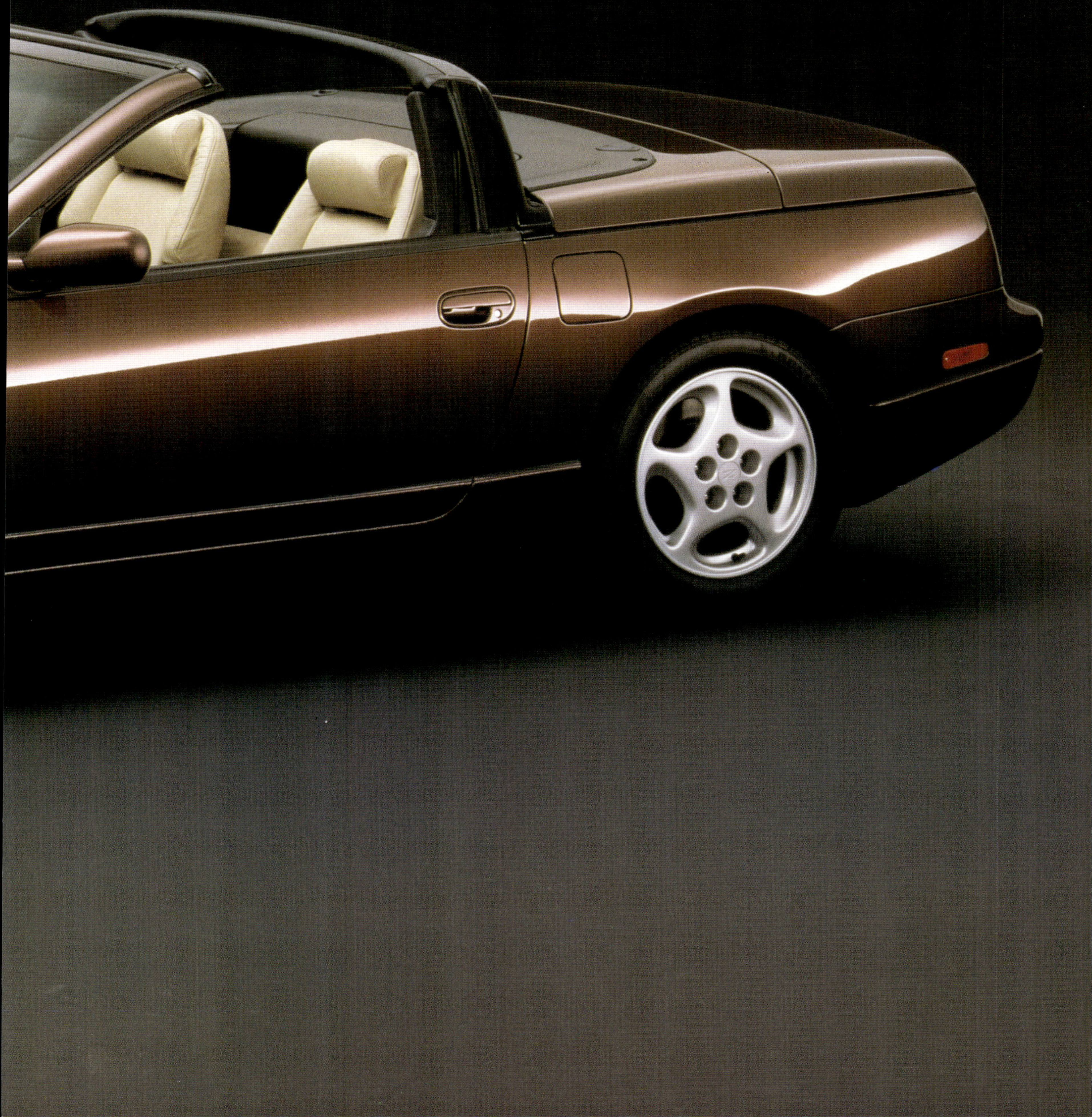

108 CLASSIC CONVERTIBLES

Previous pages: New during 1992 was the Nissan 300ZX convertible. Under the sleek styling was a 24-valve V6 engine of 2960cc, giving 230bhp.

Left: What the USA knew as a Geo Metro, other markets knew as a Suzuki Swift, and the Japanese domestic market knew as a Suzuki Cultus. The Swift range of small cars had engines of 1 to 1.3 liters, and made excellent 'fun' cars.

Below left: Introduced in 1992, the Nissan 240SX convertible had a 2389cc 16-valve four-cylinder engine offering 155bhp and a power-operated convertible top.

Below right: The Mazda Carol roll-top's original three-cylinder, 12-valve engine of just 550cc was built by Suzuki and put out 40bhp; the model illustrated is a later 660 version, with a larger engine.

Right: Honda's cheeky Beat was announced in 1991. The car had a tiny fuel-injected three-cylinder engine.

Below right: With the Mazda MX-5 of 1989 (also known as the Miata), elements of several European two-seaters of the 1960s were copied and combined with modern technology to produce a superb and affordable open sportscar.

Overleaf: Suzuki's 1991 Cappuccino two-seater had a 657cc three-cylinder engine, turbocharged and intercooled to give 64bhp and a maximum speed of 93mph.

Mazda's MX-5 Miata of 1989 was designed to have the appeal of a 1960s European open two-seater, but remained unique among Japanese products, while the Nissan Infiniti M30, based on the company's Leopard coupe and introduced in 1989, was intended solely for the American market.

Modern 'Fun' Cars

During the 1980s Japanese manufacturers became very good at creating 'fun' cars, aimed mainly at young city-dwellers; inevitably, many of these were open models. Among the first was Honda's City convertible, designed by Pininfarina in Italy and based on the City hatchback. Mazda was later successful with its cheeky Autozam Carol of 1989 and its 121 of 1990, both of which had folding roofs reminiscent of those on the small French sedans of the early 1950s. Also noteworthy was Suzuki's Swift, which remained a small sedan for most markets, but which could be purchased after 1990 in convertible form as the Geo Metro in the United States, where it was built by a subdivision of Chevrolet.

Toward the end of the 1980s a whole series of 'retrocars' appeared, intended mainly for the Japanese home market. These were models which were meant to evoke nostalgic memories of earlier vehicles, but which incorporated modern technology. Among them, although aimed at an international market, was the 1989 Mazda Miata two-seater sportscar. More typical was the 1989 Nissan Figaro (a coupe with opening roof), while the Honda Beat and Suzuki Cappuccino two-seater convertibles revealed fertile imaginations at work, and may well herald a new type of affordable open car to come from Japan.

Index

Page numbers in *italics* refer to illustrations.

Alfa Romeo 62, 66, 72
  prewar 6C-2500 72
  1954 1900 Super Sport 67
  1950s Giulia GTC *65*
  1955 Giulietta spyder *63*, 67
  1958 2000 spyder *62*, 67, 72
  1966 Duetto 67
  1970s, 1990s Montreal, SZ 72
Alvis 33
  1950s TC21/100 drophead *20-21*
  1950s TD21 33
  1965 TE21 drophead *27*
AMC 1985 Alliance 86
Armstrong Siddeley 33
  1950s Hurricane drophead *8-9*
Aston Martin 35
  1948 DB1 *10*
  1964 DB5 drophead *12*, *26*
  1990 Zagato supercar *35*
Audi Quattro Treser *47*
Austin Atlantic 22
Austin-Healey 28, 101
  1962 3000 Mark II *6-7*, *26*
  1964 Sprite 26
Auto Union 42, *43*

Bentley 22, 35
  1956 S-type *24*
BMW 42, 44, 48
  1950s 501, 502, 503 *38*, 44
  1956-59 507 48
  1961 700 42, *42*
  1967 1600 cabriolet 42
  1970s-80s 3-series 42, 44, *45-47*
  1988-89 Z1 *17*, *46*, 48
Borgward 38, 42
  1949 1.5-liter 1500 41
  1952 1800, 1955 Isabella 42
Bugatti, Ettore 52
Bugatti cars, company 52
  1940s/1950s Type 57/Type 101 52, *52*
Buick 86
  1947 convertible *76*

Cadillac 81, *84*, 86
  1950s convertible *4-5*
  1950s-70s Eldorado 81-82, 86, *90-91*
  1986-90 Allanté *18*, *92*, *93*
Chevrolet 86
  1950s-80s Corvette *13*, 76, *80*, 81, 86, 88, *92*
  1957 Bel Air *82*
  1962 Corvair 84, *87*
  1967 Camaro 81, *92*, 92
  1990s Geo Metro *100*, 108, *108*
Chrysler 86
  1948 Town and Country *78-79*
Citroën 58
  1948 2CV sedan 52, 58
  1950s/60s DS *50-51*, 53, 58

Daihatsu cars *104*, 105
Daimler (UK) 22, 33, 35
Datsun 96
  1959 Fairlady S211 *96*, 101
  1962 SPL310 *96*, 101
  1965/67 1600/2000 sports 101
  1982 280SZ turbo *98-99*
DKW sedan-based convertible 42
Dodge,
  1970 Challenger *89*
  1990 Shadow 86

Excalibur 81

1980s Series V Phaeton *93*
Facel Metallon bodywork 52, 53, *53*, *54*, 58
Facel Vega 52, 54
  1961 Facellia *54*
Ferrari, Enzo 72
Ferrari company 66
  1950s-60s 250GT spyder *12*
  1966 365 spyder California *64*
  1969 Daytona spyder *15*, *60-61*
  1979 400i *72*
  1984 Mondial cabriolet *73*
Fiat 62, 66, 101
  1940s Millecento 62, 66
  types 500, 600, 850 66, 67
  1959 Fiat-Osca 1500S 67
  1963 1500 cabriolet *63*
  1965 850 spyder 66, 66
  1966 124 spyder 67, *67*
  1967 Dino 67
  1973 X1/9 Targa top 67, 101
  1979 Ritmo (Strada) 67
Ford 18, 52, 84
  1950s Thunderbird 42, 76, 81, *83*, 88
  1950s Fairline 500 Skyliner 84
  1950s Zodiac *24*, 26
  1948-65 Lincoln Continental 76, 84, 87
  1950s-60s Zephyr *11*, *27*, 33
  1950s-60s Consul 33
  1959 Galaxie Skyliner *74-75*, 85
  1963 Falcon 84
  1964 Mustang 81, 88, *88*, 92
  1980s Escort *34*, 35, 42

Hebmüller conversion 41
Hillman Minx 33
Honda 96
  1960s S500, S600 105
  1960s S800 *97*, 105
  1980s City convertible 108
  1980s-90s CRX 105, *105*
  1990s Beat 108, *109*
Humber 1949-50 Supersnipe *11*, 35

Jaguar 26, 28, 35
  1948 XK120 *25*, 26
  1960s-1970s E-type *1*, 26, *31*
  1983 XJ-S Targa top 32, *33*, 35
Jensen 30, 35

Kaiser-Darrin 1954 roadster 86
Karmann Beetle conversion *40*, 41
Karmann-Ghia car 42, *43-44*

Lagonda 23, 35
Lancia 62, 66
  1955 Aurelia B24 *66*, 67
  1957 Appia cabriolet 67
  1960 Flaminia GT *62*, 67, *67*
  1974 Beta spyder 67
Lea Francis 1980 3.5-liter *16*
Lincoln Continental 76, 84, 87
Lotus,
  1960s Lotus 7 26
  1968, 1989 Elan 28, *30*, 101

Maserati 66, 72
  1967 Ghibli *68-69*
  1984 Biturbo coupe *70-71*
Mazda,
  1989 MX-5 Miata *101*, 108, *109*
  1989 Autozam Carol 108, *109*
  1980s RX-7 *94-95*
  1990 121 108
Mercedes-Benz 38, 41, 42, 44, 48, 92
  1949-51 170S *7*, 41-42, 44
  1954 120SL sportscar 48
  1954 190SL sportscar *39*
  1957 300SL *13*, *39*, 48
  1950s-60s 300, 300S 44
  1960s 220SE *36-37*, *41*, 44
  1960s 300SE 44

1963 230SL, 1971 350SL 48
1989 500SL 48
1992 300CE-24 coupe 44
Messerschmitt Tiger 41
MG 22, 28, 101
  1940s YA sedan, YT tourer 33
  1962-70s MGB 26, *28*
  1964-70s Midget 26
  1992 MGB revival 28
Morris Minor *28*, 33

Nissan 96
  1980s 100NX, Pulsar NX 105
  1981 280ZX 2+2 105
  1989 Infiniti M30 108
  1989-90s Figaro *105*, 108
  1990 300ZX Targa top 105, *106-7*
  1990s 240SX 108

Oldsmobile 86, *89*
Opel 1980s Ascona, Kadett 42
Osca 66, 67

Packard 1948 Custom Eight *81*
Panhard 1952 Dyna Junior 52
Peugeot 52, 58, 84
  1940s, 1950s 202, 203 58
  1950s-60s 403 *53*, 58
  1961 404 *55*, 58
  1966 204 cabriolet *57*, 58
  1969 504 cabriolet *57*, 58
  1972 304S cabriolet 58
  1986 205 convertible 58, *58*
Pininfarina styling *15*, *55*, *57*, 58, *63-64*, *66-67*, 67, *72-73*, 93, 108
Plymouth,
  1960 Fury *85*
  1963 Valiant 84
Porsche 41, 48
  1950 356 sports coupe *38*, 48
  1960s-70s 911 Targa top *43*, 48
  1969-73 VW-Porsche 914, *42*, 48
  1980s 911 cabriolet 48, *48*
  1988 944S convertible 48
  1990 944 cabriolet *2-3*, *49*
  1991 968 convertible 48, *48*

Renault 58, 86
  1959 Floride *54*, 58
  1961 4 sedan *56*
  1962 Caravelle *57*, 58
  1991 19 cabriolet 58, *58*
Riley 2.5-liter drophead coupe 33
Rolls-Royce 22, 35
  1963 Silver Cloud III *14*
  1971 Corniche *31*
  1992 Corniche IV *34*
Rover 28
  1992 models 35
  1992 214 Honda-based 35

SAAB 900 cabriolet *17*, 18
Simca 1957 Aronde *53*, 58
Singer 1950s Gazelle 33
Sunbeam,
  1950s Rapier 33
  1955 Mark III convertible *25*
Sunbeam-Talbot 1948 drophead 33
Suzuki,
  1990s Cappuccino 108, *110*
  1990s Swift/Cultus *100*, 108, *108*
  1992 Vitara *19*, *104*

Talbot 1982 Samba 58
Toyota,
  1960s 1000 convertible 105
  1980s Celica *18*, *102-3*, 105
  1984 MR2 *100*, 105
Triumph 6, 28
  1940s 1800 roadster *23*
  1960s TR4 *14*, 26, *28*
  1962-70s Spitfire 26, *32*
  late 1960s Stag *15*
  1972 TR6 *29*
  1979 TR7 drophead *29*, 29

TVR 32
  1980s 350i *33*

Vauxhall 1980s Cavalier 35
Venture 1980s cabriolet 58, *59*
Volkswagen 38, 42, 48
  1948-49 convertible *41*, 42, 84
  1950s Karmann-Ghia *40*, 42, *43*
  1969 VW-Porsche 914 *42*, 48
  1979 Karmann Golf 42, *44*, 52, 58
Volvo 1990s 480ES cabriolet 18

Acknowledgments

The author and publisher would like to thank David Eldred for designing this book, Ron Watson for compiling the index, and Clare Haworth-Maden for editing it. The following individuals and agencies provided photographic material:

Neill Bruce, pages: 1, 8-9, 10, 16, 25 (bottom), 26, 27 (bottom), 29 (bottom), 30 (bottom), 31 (bottom), 33 (bottom), 35 (bottom), 43 (top), 45, 46-47, 68-69, 72, 73
Neill Bruce/Nigel Dawes, pages: 6-7
Neill Bruce/Sven Eric Deler, pages: 59 (top), 83 (top)
Neill Bruce/Tobjorn Hansson, page: 92 (top)
Neill Bruce/Peter Haventon, page: 81 (top)
Neill Bruce/The Midland Motor Museum, Bridgnorth, pages: 13 (top), 28 (middle)
Neill Bruce/The Peter Roberts Collection, pages: 11 (bottom), 19, 20-21, 22, 24 (top), 34 (both), 35 (top), 40-41 (bottom), 56 (bottom), 70-71, 81 (bottom), 86 (top), 92 (middle and bottom), 94-95, 104, 105 (top and bottom right), 106-107, 108 (all three), 109 (bottom), 110-111
Neill Bruce/Nicky Wright, pages: 65, 89 (top), 90-91, 93 (bottom)
Colin Burnham, pages: 4-5, 13 (bottom), 82, 84, 96 (bottom)
David Hodges, pages: 18, 29 (top), 32 (bottom), 33 (top), 57 (top), 76-77 (both), 86-87
Life File/Ford Motor Company, page: 88
Life File/Guy Usher, pages: 12 (top), 46, 109 (top)
Andrew Morland, pages: 15 (bottom), 17 (bottom), 23 (top), 28 (top), 40, 47 (top), 64 (both), 66 (top and bottom), 67 (bottom)
National Motor Museum, Beaulieu, England, pages: 2-3, 14 (bottom), 15 (top), 17 (top), 18 (bottom), 23 (middle and bottom), 24 (bottom), 27 (top), 28 (bottom), 30 (top), 31 (top), 32 (bottom), 36-37, 38 (both), 39 (both), 42 (all three), 43 (bottom), 44, 52, 53 (both), 54 (both), 55, 56 (top), 57 (bottom), 58 (both), 62 (both), 63 (both), 66 (middle), 67 (bottom), 68 (bottom), 82-83, 96 (top), 97, 98-99, 100 (top), 102-103
The James L Taylor Collection, pages: 7, 59 (bottom), 105 (bottom left)
James Taylor/Porsche, pages: 48 (top), 48-49, 49 (top)
J Winkley, pages: 14 (top), 25 (top), 40-41 (top)
N Wright/National Motor Museum, pages: 11 (top), 12 (bottom), 50-51, 60-61, 67 (top), 68 (top), 74-75, 78-79, 80, 85 (both), 87 (top), 89 (bottom), 93 (top), 100 (bottom), 101